Dedication

This book is dedicated to some men of God who have inspired me over the years and continue to do so: Arthur Blessitt, Gerald Coates, Billy Graham, Norman Barnes, Ishmael, J. John and Jeff Lucas - my spiritual heroes and most of them my friends too.

> *"But life is worth nothing unless I use it for doing the work assigned me by the Lord Jesus - the work of telling others the good news about God's mighty kindness and love."*
> *Acts 20:24*

Making
Friends
Evangelism the Easy Way

Steve Legg

Silver Fish
creative marketing

Published in Great Britain 1998 by
Silver Fish Creative Marketing.

British Library Cataloguing in Publication Data
A record for this book is available from the British Library

ISBN 1 902134 01 X

Printed and bound in Great Britain by
Cox & Wyman Ltd, Reading, Berks.

Silver Fish Creative Marketing Ltd
44c Fermoy Road, Maida Vale
London W9 3NH

Contents

About the Author

Steve Legg was born and grew up in Bournemouth. He became a Christian in his early teens through his involvement with the Boys' Brigade. After leaving school at the age of sixteen, Steve entered the banking profession where he embarked on a very successful career until, at the age of twenty one, God called him into full-time evangelism. Steve trained on a Pioneer TIE (Training In Evangelism) Team in 1988 for a year, and since that time has worked as an itinerant evangelist.

He often uses his skills as an escapologist to draw and entertain large crowds, before communicating the freedom that a relationship with Jesus brings. Steve takes this powerful message into schools, colleges, universities, prisons, pubs, night clubs and out onto the streets - in fact, wherever people are.

As a Guinness World Record holder, Steve travels the length and breadth of the country, as well as working in various countries across the world. He has been privileged to work with a whole list of household names, including Jonathan Ross, Fern Britton, Paul Ross, Helen Shapiro, Gloria Gaynor, Boyzone, Roger Whittaker, Zoe Ball, Keith Chegwin and Lorraine Chase, to name just a few!

Dangerous and exciting escapes suspended from cranes, or manacled between two high powered jeeps going in opposite directions have also brought major media attention to Steve's abilities. He has appeared on national television on numerous occasions, and his impressive list of TV credits include: *How 2*, *The Big Breakfast*, and *The Disney Club*, right through to *Songs of Praise*.

Steve continues to be a major contributor at all the major Christian festivals and events, including Spring Harvest, Grapevine, Eurofest, The Event, Summer Madness, Cross Rhythms, Firm Foundations and Kingdom Faith, and in 1995 was part of *The Cannon and Ball Gospel Show* that toured the UK. This major tour covered a staggering 48 dates across the nation, making it one of the biggest Gospel tours ever produced, and was the subject of a BBC special documentary, and became the number one best-seller video of its kind.

Steve is married to Jemma, and has two small children, Jay and Amber. He is a member of the Evangelical Alliance, London's prestigious Magic Circle and a very proud member of The Curry Club.

Thanks

To my beautiful wife Jemma: thanks darling for understanding (well most of the time anyway!) when I had to keep disappearing down to my office at the end of the garden to write, and to my wonderful children, Jay and Amber. I pray you'll be more effective witnesses than daddy ever was.

Huge thanks to some of my most loyal prayer partners and supporters: Paul Archer, Allan and Mary Botting, Jonathan and Liz, Mark and Sarah McClelland, David, Meg, Matt, Tom and K.J. Pritchard, Steve and Lyn Burnhope, Marie Brook, Steve and Cilla Sparks, Steve and Luz Gale, Jim and Pat Tweeddale, Guy and Bev Fortescue, Will and Clare Palmer and certainly not forgetting Andy Economides - thanks for believing in me and what I do.

To the lads from the Boys' Brigade: if it wasn't for you I probably wouldn't be writing this: Ken Bradley, Graham King, Duggie Dugdale, Roy Stacey, and of course Geoff Micklefield (thanks for all those pancakes and the chats), who helped me stick with Christianity in the early days when I thought about giving it all up.

To the Patron of my trust, Lord David Alton of Liverpool, and my Council of Reference: Steve Chalke, J. John, Jeff Lucas, Wynne Lewis, Roger Ellis, Gerald Coates, Canon Brian Phillips and Phil Wall. Thanks for all your advice, availability and encouragement.

To all those people whose homes I've stayed in and have looked after me so well, especially the Pritchards in Buxton (keep baking those chocolate crispy treats), Gary and Joanne Faulkener from Bangor, Northern Ireland (your Ulster Fry's are simply the best Joanne), Cliff and Jen Needs down on the farm in Wellington, Somerset and Micky Boy, Karen, Treena and Jason Hornsey who look after me so well each time I'm in Bristol.

Whilst I'm on the subject of travel, a big shout to the gang who have come out with me on the road; notably James Clark (JC), Danny (Wedgwood) Raywood, Andy Webb (The Webbster), Billy Lincoln (Big Billy), "Mad" Matt Smith, Nathan (Locket) Lock, Rob Smith (The Robster) and the intrepid TIE Teamers, Carlos, Nico, Thomas, Kerry, Amanda, Emily and Jackie - thanks to you all.

And of course to Ishy and Irene, my great friends, Andy and Joy Clark aka Doublecheck (we've had some great times together) - they're the best, and to Chris Gidney, Tommy Cannon and Bobby Ball.

Also, huge thanks to my publishers Silver Fish, for sharing in the vision.

Foreword

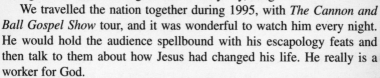

I don't usually write forewords for books, but one of the main reasons I've decided to write this one is because I know the author personally.

He is a big man, standing well over 6 feet tall, but his nature is one of gentleness and kindness. He is the proverbial gentle giant. When one meets Steve one can see Jesus working through him. He is also a good friend. Anyway, I digress ...

We travelled the nation together during 1995, with *The Cannon and Ball Gospel Show* tour, and it was wonderful to watch him every night. He would hold the audience spellbound with his escapology feats and then talk to them about how Jesus had changed his life. He really is a worker for God.

Steve is not just a person who talks about evangelism, he actually gets on and does it. He talks about his saviour in schools, in prisons, out on the streets, on the radio and TV. In fact, anywhere he can get an ear to listen.

The other reason that I recommend *Making Friends* is because I know it makes sense. God changed my life in a big way, and I tell people about it. But I know that there are some who don't find evangelising easy. In fact they find it very difficult to share their faith with others, so a book like this is great news!

I hope this book will give people inspiration, hope and strength to spread the wonderful message of God, and that many will be saved as a result.

Bobby Ball

Introduction

An interesting and highly strategic chain of events started in the USA in 1858, when a Sunday School teacher, Mr. Kimball, led a Boston shoe clerk to give his life to Jesus.

The clerk, a certain Dwight L. Moody, became an evangelist. In England in 1879, he stirred evangelistic passion and vision in the heart of Frederick B. Meyer, leader of a small church.

F.B. Meyer, preaching to an American college campus, saw a student named J. Wilbur Chapman become a Christian.

Chapman, working for the YMCA, employed a former baseball player, Billy Sunday, to do evangelistic work.

Billy Sunday went on to hold large Gospel meetings, including one in Charlotte, North Carolina. A group of local Christian businessmen were so enthusiastic after the meeting that they planned another evangelistic mission in their town, this time bringing a strong, rugged evangelist called Dr. Mordecai Fowler Ham to preach.

During one of Ham's meetings, a sixteen-year-old farm boy from the rural southern United States of America, named William Jefferson Graham Jr., heard the Gospel and became a Christian. Billy Graham, as he became better known, subsequently attended the Bob Jones College in Cleveland and the Florida Bible Institute near Tampa where he began preaching in 1938 and was ordained a year later as a southern Baptist minister.

Graham's reputation as an evangelist grew steadily during and immediately after the second world war, as a result of his radio broadcasts, tent revivals and featured appearances at George W. Wilson's "Youth for Christ" rallies in the United States and Great Britain. He has gone on to become recognised as the 20th Century's most successful evangelist, who through his Gospel crusades is estimated to have seen 3m men, women and children respond at his meetings across the world.

In 1985, for example, Billy Graham's Global Mission was broadcast to 185 countries, and his message was translated into 100 different languages. Never in human history did so many people hear the Gospel preached on the same day. This Global Mission was heard in at least 2,000 venues. The Sony Corporation has said that the Betacam equipment set-up ordered by the mission organisers was the largest ever, surpassing the Olympics and even the World Cup!

Billy's syndicated newspaper column, "My Answer" is carried by newspapers with a combined circulation of 5 million. *Decision* magazine, published by his own organisation, is read in 158 countries and has a circulation of nearly 2 million.

Billy Graham has preached to more people in live addresses than anyone else in history. Over 180 million have heard him in 180 countries and territories. Even greater numbers have been reached through television, radio, video and film. Dr Graham has commented: "My one purpose in life is to help people find a personal relationship with God which, I believe, comes through knowing Christ."

Inspiring stuff, but you might feel you're not cut out to be the next Billy Graham. Well, so what! You could be someone like a Mr Kimball, who started the whole process off, by simply telling a few others what God had done in his life. Only eternity will reveal the tremendous impact of that one Sunday School teacher, Mr Kimball, who told others of the good news of Jesus. Why shouldn't it be the same for us?

Making Friends isn't some major theological tome, it's certainly not intended as that. It's simply a little book that aims to make evangelism a little bit easier so we can all do a little bit more of it.

> *"I am not ashamed of the Gospel because it is the power of God, for the salvation of everyone who believes."*
> *(Romans 1:16)*

1: Just an Ordinary Person

Many people don't do evangelism because they think they're not special enough, they don't read their Bibles for long enough, or don't pray for hours on end. Come on, if we're honest I'm sure we can all say those things - I know I certainly can. But the good news is this: God loves to use ordinary people who feel they don't qualify.

General Eisenhower once rebuked one of his Generals for referring to a soldier as "just a Private". He reminded him that the army could function better without its Generals than it could without its foot soldiers. "If this war is won," he said, "it will be won by Privates." If the Gospel is to be taken to the lost, it will be us "ordinary" Christians who will do it.

The Bible tells us a wonderful story about a man named "Ananias - a Christian in Damascus" - that's all he was called, not a terribly auspicious title was it? He was just a normal Christian who was available to God, who went on to be used in an incredible way.

There was a follower of Jesus in Damascus named Ananias. The Lord spoke to him in a vision: "Ananias!" Ananias answered, "Here I am Lord." The Lord said to him, "Get up and go to Straight Street. Find the house of Judas, and ask for a man named Saul from the city of Tarsus. He is there now, praying. Saul has seen a vision in which a man named Ananias comes to him and lays his hands on him. Then he is able to see again."

But Ananias answered, "Lord, many people have told me about this man and the terrible things he did to your holy people in Jerusalem. Now he has come here to Damascus, and the leading priests have given him the power to arrest everyone who worships you."

*But the Lord said to Ananias, "Go! I have chosen Saul for an impor-
tant work. He must tell about me to those who are not Jews, to kings and
to the people of Israel. I will show him how must he must suffer for my
name."*

*So Ananias went to the house of Judas. He laid his hands on Saul and
said, "Brother Saul, the Lord Jesus sent me. He is the one you saw on the
road on your way here. He sent me so that you can see again and be filled
with the Holy Spirit." Immediately, something that looked like fish scales
fell from Saul's eyes, and he was able to see again! Then Saul got up and
was baptised. After he ate some food, his strength returned (Acts 9:10-19).*

Powerful stuff. Let's look a little closer and see how significant the
whole episode was and Ananias's essential role in probably the most
famous conversion story in history.

Paul, who before his conversion was known as Saul, started off as an
enemy of Christians. He had been persecuting them in Jerusalem and was
on his way to Damascus to extradite others. The journey was made on
foot and took about a week. Saul's only companions were the officers of
the Sanhedrin, a kind of police force. Because he was a Pharisee, he could
have nothing to do with them, so he walked by himself, and probably
thought a great deal, as there was nothing else to do.

His route took him through Galilee, which probably brought thoughts
of Jesus back to his mind. So he came near Damascus, one of the oldest
cities in the world. As he finished his 140 mile journey and was on the
outskirts of the city, a bright light from Heaven suddenly flashed around
him, and Jesus spoke to Saul. He immediately surrendered his life to
Jesus and entered Damascus a changed man, with these instructions: "Get
up and go into the city. Someone there will tell you what you must do."

There's no prizes for guessing who that someone was. Yes, good old
Ananias, whom I believe to be one of the forgotten heroes of the early
Church. God spoke to Ananias, and told him that he must go and see Saul;
he is even directed to the right street and the right house!

Ananias must have thought he was going stark staring mad! Saul was
known as a murderer of Christians - there probably wasn't a man living or
dead who he was more afraid of, and here was God telling Ananias to go
and speak with him. God even told him why he must go, and two reasons
were given: first, that Saul was already praying and was now ready, and sec-
ondly, that he had been shown a vision of Ananias coming to pray for him.

God was arranging what I like to call a "divine appointment", and they most definitely still work today. Myself and a small team had been visiting Paris, working with a Tamil church and doing evangelism, mainly in the form of street theatre and the like. It was our night off, and my friend Andy, who was working with an inner-city church in Tooting, and I decided to go up the Eiffel Tower. We'd had a good look around, and prayed that God would give us one of these divine appointments.

Coming back down in the crowded lift, I felt a real compulsion to preach the Gospel - I figured I'd have a stationary audience for a good two minutes - so I did it! It all seemed to go down well, and we struck up a conversation with a guy from New Zealand who was on holiday. He was impressed with what we'd been sharing, and asked where we went to church because he was currently living in the UK and, would you believe it, in Tooting, less than five minutes walk away from where my mate Andy lived. Now that's what I call a divine appointment!

So, back to the story, with another divine appointment. You see, it had to be Ananias who spoke to Saul. If Ananias had opted out and had sent his mate Keith or Barry instead (no irreverence intended here!), it just wouldn't have tied up with Saul's vision. I hope I'm making the point here that Ananias was the only man for this job. In our situations too we are often the right people for the job.

On a personal level, I can reach people you can't. I have the great privilege of working with various show business personalities from time to time. Only a little time ago, I flew to Glasgow to appear on a well-known children's TV programme and had a great time chatting with the presenters, all well-known celebrities in their own right. We just clicked, and I found it all so natural.

I also have had opportunities, through some mainstream work I do with a major brewery, to get to know and befriend a number of the countries top "blue" comedians. In fact, one of them, who earns a lot of money doing very adult humour, went with me for a drink and a curry, and I had the wonderful privilege of praying for him to become a Christian.

Now you might feel totally inadequate about witnessing to these sort of people, but I feel at home and relaxed with them. However, I would feel totally out of my depth with some of your friends, and the folk that you relate to. Do you see what I'm getting at? We're all in a unique position with certain people.

As we can see in our story, God went on to reassure Ananias by showing him how He was going to use Saul. This is another useful point from the story and something I do a lot. I try to see what I call "God potential" in people, and how God might use them if they became Christians. I tell you, it really does help, and it certainly gets you praying.

I was leading an evangelism training session in Holland some years back and was teaching about this very principle. I'd also been working out on the streets, just outside Amsterdam, performing and speaking. There was this guy called Dennis, and he was giving me a bit of a hard time, so in one session I used Dennis as an illustration. I was telling them that he'd make a great evangelist because he had such a loud mouth! Once I had said that, I thought I'd better pray that he actually did become a Christian, and praise God, by the end of the weekend Dennis got saved. So there, it does work.

Back to the story for the last time. Did you notice Ananias's first words to Saul? I'm positive he was filled with terror and fear on his way to his rendezvous with Saul in Straight Street. But the book of Acts tells us that his opening two words were, "Brother Saul". What a welcome, friendly and warm. What good news too, from a very ordinary person who was available to God.

For me, this availability started at a Gary Glitter concert! *The Leader's Gang Show* had come to town on New Year's Eve, 1987 for a massive party. After the chimes at midnight, when I'd shaken a few hands and kissed a few cheeks in the customary manner, I prayed with all my heart, "God, I'll do anything for you this year and beyond, whatever you want, I'll do it, just tell me what you want me to do". And I really meant it. No booming voices from Heaven or anything like that, but the process had started.

I've got to tell you, nothing happened for months. I couldn't figure if God wanted me to stay where I was working and be 'salt and light' there, be a missionary in deepest Peru, or indeed anything in between! My friends from church, Jonathan and Liz, were really helpful and we talked a lot about guidance. They suggested praying and fasting, so that's what I struggled with, every Wednesday for four months.

Then, one night at Spring Harvest in Minehead, where I was working as a steward, God called me. He told me, so that I knew without any shadow of doubt, that He was calling me to be an evangelist. I went home fired up, told my parents (who weren't Christians) that I was leaving my well-paid career with Barclays Bank to actually pay to be trained on a Pioneer Evangelistic Training Initiative for a year. Well, to say that they blew their tops would be the understatement of the decade! They were absolutely furious, and for a period of six solid months I suffered all sorts of emotional blackmail and disapproval. The other "minor" problem was that I was a very shy and insecure person. The thought of standing up in front of just a handful of people would so cripple me with fear that I would make myself physically ill. But deep down I knew God had called me, and I went on to be obedient to that call.

Since that time I have had the privilege of travelling the length and breadth of the UK, with visits to France, Switzerland, Holland, Norway and the USA, speaking to large crowds about my faith. I have spoken face to face with hundreds of thousands of teenagers, as I have visited schools and colleges across Europe, including a quarter of all the secondary schools in Northern Ireland. I have spoken with many top television personalities and well-known names, including working with Keith Chegwin and the Rt. Hon. and Most Reverend George Carey, Archbishop of Canterbury in one week alone! I have had opportunities to reach millions with the Gospel and seen literally a few thousand people get saved. I'm not telling you these things to show you how great I am, but to show you how great the grace of God is. I know if He can use me, He can use anyone.

2: Why Do We?

I mentioned in the last chapter how I got into evangelism, but let me backtrack a little first. For me, it all started in a field in Sidmouth, Devon. I had joined the Boys' Brigade - the 7th Bournemouth Company to be precise. I thoroughly enjoyed the activities and the social side of it but church was a bit of a drag - well, the one we had to go to was anyway. It seemed dead, as though it should have been buried 50 years ago! All that God stuff was way above my head, until we went off for summer camp in Devon.

During the camp, the leaders talked about Jesus as if He were still alive and we were all given a little book called *Journey Into Life*. Well, I read and read it again, and then re-read it, just to be sure! It was a revelation to me, that God loved me and could change my life. I decided that if this was true, then I most definitely wanted it. I thought about this all the way back on the coach and when I got home I dumped my suitcase in the kitchen, ran up to my bedroom, got on my knees and prayed the prayer of committment with all my heart.

I was now a Christian. The book mentioned that it would be a good idea to tell someone what I had just done, within 24-hours, so I went downstairs and told my dad. I'll never forget his first words when I told him about my new life: "What have you done a stupid (in fact rather stronger words to that effect!) thing like that for!" I'm pleased to say that didn't put me off, but made me more determined to live as a Christian and to tell others, and become somewhat more successful at it too, I might add.

We've seen earlier how Saul was converted and how he became Paul the great missionary. He met Jesus, fell in love with Him and dedicated his life to telling the glorious message of the Gospel. To Paul, the Gospel was a cause for glory. It wasn't just a nice theory, it was a powerful truth. Indeed, one that he had lived for more than twenty years. The Gospel worked, it was true and as far as he was concerned was for everyone.

So now was the time for him to visit the Roman church, but before he went he wanted the Christians in Rome to understand what he believed. *"I have a duty to all people - Greeks and those who are not Greeks, the wise and the foolish. That is why I want so much to preach the Good News to you in Rome.*

"I am proud of the Good News, because it is the power God uses to save everyone who believes - to save the Jews first, and also to save those who are not Jews. The Good News shows how God makes people right with himself - that it begins and ends with faith. As the Scripture says, 'But those who are right with God will live by trusting in him'" (Romans 1:14-17).

I read an interesting article in a newspaper entitled "Conversion to Hindu Faith Is Tortuous". The article stated: "A German businessman has completed his conversion to the Hindu faith by piercing himself through the cheeks with an inch thick, 4 foot-long steel rod, and pulling a chariot for 2 miles by ropes attached to his back and chest by steel hooks. Others walk through 20 foot-long pits of fire, wear shoes with soles made of nails, or hang in the air spread eagled from hooks embedded in their backs".

Not a bundle of laughs is it? Aren't you glad that conversion to Christianity isn't like that? What we as Christians have to communicate is not merely good advice, it is good news! If you have some good news you just don't want to keep it to yourself, you want to tell others. I was present when my daughter Amber was born and what an experience that was. Although it was late at night, there I was, the proud father, straight on the mobile phone telling people, faxing friends in South Africa - it would have been selfish to have kept it to ourselves.

In the same way, Jesus never intended that we should keep the good news of God all to ourselves. Just as He was sent to earth by his Father, so He sent His disciples: *"As the Father sent me, I now send you"* (John 20:21). That's what the Gospel is like. The word "Gospel" literally means good news, that Jesus died so that we might become friends with God, have abundant life, know forgiveness, have a purpose for living, and to have a heavenly Dad who's perfect. The Gospel is good news of great joy to those who are lonely, lost and unforgiven.

I was speaking and performing in the north of France with a small evangelistic team, and we had a great time, reaching many young people and making loads of friends along the way. As was our usual practice, the team leader and I used to wander down the road each night for chips and mayonnaise - our little treat! Because he had seen us about town, the guy serving us asked what we were doing and why we were there. "Business or pleasure?" he enquired. "A little of both," was the team leader's response. I couldn't believe that this potential opportunity had been missed. We have a duty to tell others, it would be wrong not to, so let's not miss any chance that comes our way, even if we are a bit peckish at the particular time.

The Gospel is described in so many different ways in the Bible, and has many facets. It's the good news of:

1. Salvation - *"When you heard the true teaching - the Good News about your salvation - you believed in Christ"* (Ephesians 1:13).

2. Reconciliation - *"Through the Good News those who are not Jews will share with Jews in God's blessing"* (Ephesians 3:6).

3. Peace - *"On your feet wear the Good News of peace to help you stand strong"* (Ephesians 6:15).

4. Hope - *"You must not be moved away from the hope brought to you by the Good News that you heard"* (Colossians 1:23).

5. Jesus - *"Remember Jesus Christ, who was raised from the dead, who is from the family of David. This is the Good News I preach"* (Timothy 2:8).

The Greek word for Gospel, "euangelion", was originally used as a term to describe the message brought back announcing a victory in battle. For us it's a wonderful declaration of what God has done for us through Jesus - the announcement of the greatest victory the world has ever known.

One of the world's most successful fast-food companies is Domino's Pizza. It is no surprise that the founder of the company has a clearly defined statement of mission. In his own words, "Domino's has a single goal. Its mission is simple: to deliver a high-quality pizza, hot, within thirty minutes at a fair price". Everything they do at Domino's, is centred on that goal.

It amazes me how passionate people get about pizza's, fizzy drinks, hamburgers and the like. I wish Christians would get so stirred up about our mission, which the Bible calls "The Great Commission". Here is a wonderful piece of scripture; and it is for us today, not just the Apostles to whom it was originally given: *"All authority in heaven and on earth has been given to me. Therefore, go and make disciples of all nations, baptising them in the name of the Father and of the Son and of the Holy Spirit, and teaching them to obey everything I have commanded you"* (Matthew 28:18-20).

It's interesting to note that earlier in His ministry Jesus had sent out the Apostles on a restricted mission: *"Go to the people of Israel, who are like lost sheep"* (Matthew 10:5-6). But now, in this day of the Great Commission He's changed Israel to "all nations" - for them and us, the Gentiles, to take the whole world for God.

In attempting to recruit John Sculley, the 38-year-old president of Pepsi-Cola, Steve Jobs, co-founder of Apple Computers, issued a tremendous challenge to Sculley. He asked: "Do you want to spend the rest of your life selling sugared water, or do want a chance to change the world?"

We might not be able to change the world, but we can certainly change someone's life. How will people hear if we don't tell them? *"God does not want anyone to be lost, but he wants all people to change their hearts and lives"* (2 Peter 3:9). Some of the people that you and I know are literally running out of time.

One night in 1962, in a hotel in Seattle, the evangelist Billy Graham was sound asleep. Suddenly he woke up with what he later described as a burden to pray for Marilyn Monroe, the movie actress. When the feeling continued the next day, one of Graham's associates tried to reach the actress through her agent. The agent offered no hope for a meeting immediately. "Not now, maybe two weeks from now," he said.

Two weeks later Marilyn Monroe's suicide shocked the world. Two weeks was too late. God has left the job in our hands, so let's go forward and get on with it before it's too late.

3: Why Don't We?

I'm passionate about my football team, Brighton and Hove Albion, and I can talk to total strangers down my local pub about their results and their abilities on the pitch with no problem at all. But, when it comes to striking up a conversation about Christianity, well, then I start to get a bit hot under the collar - and evangelism is my job! It's funny isn't it? We seem to have no problem talking about the weather, or football and things that don't really matter, but when it comes to talking to others about our faith we start to panic a bit. But why is this? Here's my top five reasons:

1. Fear of how people might react
2. Not knowing what to say
3. People might ask us tough questions we can't answer
4. Worries of what people might think about us
5. A confused view of what evangelism and witnessing involve

I'm going to be looking at all these issues in this book, but the real big one is fear, so let's look at it first.

Fear is not a problem that stops just Christians from getting on with their job. During the second world war, a military governor met with General George Patton in Sicily. When the governor praised Patton highly for his courage and bravery, Patton replied, "Sir, I am not a brave man - the truth is, I am an utter coward. I have never been within the sound of gunshot or in the sight of battle in my whole life without being so scared that I had sweat in the palms of my hands." Years later, when Patton's autobiography was published, it contained the significant statement by the general: "I learned very early in my life never to take counsel of my fears."

Then there's one of my heroes, in case you hadn't already guessed, Billy Graham, whose hands often go clammy and his knees shake before he preaches. Whilst many would agree that standing in front of a crowd of people is probably not their favourite occupation, this is not a confession you would expect from a man who has preached the Gospel to more people than anyone in history. It is, however, a confession that should encourage us.

In Billy's own words: "Every time I stand before a crowd I feel so unworthy to preach the Gospel. I feel fearful that I may say something or do something that may mislead someone, because I'm talking to eternal souls who have the possibility of living in Heaven forever."

We look in the Bible at one of Jesus' best friends, Peter, the very man who on the night that Jesus died denied three times that he even knew Jesus. Yet, on the day of Pentecost he preached and 3,000 people became Christians.

Paul told the Christians in Corinth, *"I come to you with fear and trembling."* But he carries on, *"My message and my preaching were not with wise and powerful words, but with a demonstration of the Spirit's power, so that your faith might not rest on men's wisdom, but on God's power"* (1 Corinthians 2: 3-5).

Fear shouldn't disqualify us. The best antidote to fear is love. *"God's perfect love drives out all fear"* (1 John 4:18). In 1988, I spent one of the best years of my life training on a Pioneer TIE (Training in Evangelism) Team. I knew God had called me to be an evangelist. I so much wanted to do schools and street work, and to talk to large crowds, but was paralysed by fear - fear of getting it wrong, of what others might think, of looking a right idiot. My friend, Pete, whom I spent the year travelling with, prayed a great big dose of the love of God into my life, and it worked.

Since that time, I have gone on to speak to hundreds and even thousands at a time, and have on different occasions appeared on "live" TV, performing and often explaining the good news of the Gospel to millions in one go. But I still get nervous. Let's face it, we all do, and I believe that's a good thing. Nervousness tends to get the adrenaline flowing and helps you rely on God and pray more. But I don't allow fear to stop me from going into places and using God given opportunities to reach people. I'm not telling you these things to blow my own trumpet, but to show you how the love of God can change and use anyone. And always remember that *"God did not give us a spirit of fear, but a spirit of power, love and self-control"* (2 Timothy 1:7).

Very recently, I faced a rather frightening proposition. I had enjoyed a great weekend of evangelistic events in Bristol, from speaking at a dinner for ladies from a church's mums and toddlers group, through to appearing at University events and a number of visits into junior school assemblies. Things were going well, until my friends, Nigel and Mick, mentioned that our next "port of call" could be a bit tricky. They had booked me to do three double-lessons in a tough secondary school on a major estate in Bristol, a place where riots had happened a few years back. Now, I've been into tough schools, but this was something else. In fact, only a couple of weeks earlier, some glaziers had been replacing broken windows at the school. Returning to their van, which had been parked in the school car park, they found the wheels gone and the van resting on piles of bricks!

I thought maybe it might be better inside, but it wasn't. Many of the classes had two teachers, to try to maintain discipline, and some of the pupils were physically pushing staff around, and swearing at them. But amazingly, when I started talking about Jesus and the Gospel, and how much I disliked "religion", they were with me. My message went down a storm and I even got out in one piece! That evening, we had a concert to finish my visit in style. Over 250 teenagers turned up, and at the end of the evening, as I invited people to become Christians, more than 40 responded, including a handful from the school. Some of them crying their eyes out as they repented before God - it was quite a sight.

Without doubt, evangelism works. But you will often hear people say, "Evangelism is only for evangelists, and not me". Well, that's wrong for starters. Evangelism isn't just for special up-front "Super Christians" - we're all important. As we've already seen, God desires to use ordinary people.

However, research does tell us that ten per cent of Christians have evangelism as their main gift. You see, evangelists are people, called of God, who enjoy evangelism and are good at it. They *"equip the saints for works of service"* (Ephesians 4:11-13), ie, they train Christians to go and get on with it. A fascinating fact is that the Greek word for "equip" is the word a fisherman used when explaining how he mended his nets to make them efficient and serviceable.

It's interesting to note that the Greek term "evangelist" was originally applied not to Christians but to slaves whose assignment was to serve along-side an army general. If their side won, his task would be to run with the news of his general's victory. The families back home would be worrying about their men fighting in the battle, but when they saw the evangelist coming they knew the battle had been won. The arrival of the evangelist always preceded the coming of the victor, and his news prepared the people for their victory celebrations. That's fascinating.

So, we don't all have evangelism as our main gift but, as I've already said, it doesn't mean that we opt out. The Bible says that we're all witnesses, without exception: *"You will be my witnesses - in Jerusalem, in all of Judea, in Samaria and in every part of the world"* (Acts 1:8).

I don't know if you've ever been to court. I have, and I found the whole process rather nerve-racking, to say the least. So much so, I dropped my notes all over the floor, and the poor clerk of the court was scrabbling around trying to pick them up. Still, it got a bit of a laugh and relieved some of the tension. As a witness, I had to tell the magistrates what happened to me, the whole story. That is the job of a witness, to tell others what has happened to them, to have a story to tell without exaggeration and without hyping the whole thing up. But we don't just witness through our words, but through our lives and actions too.

The New Testament word for witness is "martus", from which we get the English word "martyr". It means a person who is put to death for refusing to renounce a faith or belief. Now, don't panic too much here! We might not have to physically lay down our lives for Jesus and the Gospel, but we can be prepared to lay down other things for Him.

We need to ask ourselves what we are prepared to lay down and give up for God. Are we prepared to give our time or our money? How about our independence, which is a precious thing? Or what about sharing our faith when it's not terribly convenient for us? Can we do it? But don't get too depressed at the thought of giving up things. Jesus promises us much more: *"I tell you the truth, a grain of wheat must fall to the ground and die to make many seeds. But if it never dies, it remains only a single seed. Those who love their lives will lose them, but those who hate their lives in this world will keep true life for ever"* (John 12:24-25).

You see, laying down things will help our lives to match our faith. A missionary in India was once teaching the Bible to a group of Hindu ladies. Halfway through the lesson, one of the ladies got up and walked out. A short time later, she returned and listened more intently than ever. At the end of the class, the missionary asked her: "Why did you leave the meeting? Weren't you interested?" "Oh yes," the Hindu lady replied. "I was so impressed with what you had to say about Christ that I went out to ask your driver whether you really lived the way you talked. When he said you did, I hurried back so I wouldn't miss out on anything."

A true story. So, we must ask ourselves: are we good witnessess or bad witnessess? The way we live our lives will back up the things we say about our God.

4: Being Good News

Are you good news? Are you friendly? Is your church friendly? Do you have many Christian friends? Do you have many friends who aren't yet Christians? Do you try to make friends at all? Maybe we chat to neighbours, attend family reunions and get on with work colleagues, but none of that is the mark of true friendship.

In the beginning, when God created the world and in it man - the most special part - there was still something that was not quite right. What was missing? Well, the missing piece of the jigsaw was that Adam was on his own, that his relationship with God was not enough. Genesis tells us man was made for friendship and relationships. In fact, it's through these relationships with friends, family and work colleagues, that most people become Christians.

We know this partly through research conducted on why people first came to Jesus. Over 10,000 people were asked the question, "What was responsible for your coming to Christ and this church?" The results made very interesting reading:

Evangelistic Crusades	½%
Was Visited	1%
Special Need	2%
Just Walked In	3%
Special Programme	3%
Sunday School	5%
Pastor	6%
Friend or Relative	79%

Source: Institute of Church Growth, Pasadena, California 1981

These figures have tremendous implications for all Christians. They show clearly that friendships and relationships are God's major strategy for reaching the lost. If we want to see change in the world, we must live in the world. We must get out of our cosy Christian ghettos, start making friends and start being Good News.

When it comes to evangelism, many of us try the difficult things first: door-to-door work, or stopping people in the street and accosting them with a tract and a silly nervous Christian grin! A few knock backs can be pretty soul-destroying and can sometimes put Christians off doing evangelism altogether. Inviting a friend around, or out for a drink is a different matter altogether, and can bring a completely different response.

Dale Carnegie was an American lecturer, author and pioneer in the field of public speaking and the psychology of the successful personality. He wrote the international best seller *How to win friends and influence people*, and once said: "You can make more friends in two months by becoming really interested in other people than you can in two years trying to get other people interested in you." This is another way of saying that the way to make a friend is to be a friend.

Everyone needs friends, and as we spend time with them, talking about what they find important, it gives us a right, a very natural right I might add, to share what's important to us.

After leaving school at the age of sixteen, I worked for Barclays' Bank prior to going full-time into evangelism. Working in four different branches over five years I learned fairly fast, through a number of embarrassing mistakes, the best way to go about witnessing to my mates! I found that the best way was to intrigue people. That might sound a bit odd, but it worked. You see, I was "one of the lads". I enjoyed a couple of beers, but didn't need to get drunk. I went out night clubbing with them, but I didn't go round chatting all the girls up, or sleeping around. They realised too that I didn't gossip about other colleagues behind their backs. All of this really intrigued them. I was the same as them and enjoyed being with them, yet somehow different. So, instead of talking about the Lord all the time, I prayed that my workmates would come to me of their own initiative and ask questions. They all knew I was a Christian, though I'd never told any of them up front.

My mate Kevin and I used to go down to a local sports club. One night, after a good workout, we were sitting in the sauna when he asked: "How long have you been a born-again Christian?" Good opening question or what! Kev started coming to church soon after and he was just one of a handful from the bank who started coming. All of this was achieved without Bible bashing or preaching, and without getting a reputation as a religious nutcase.

I've spent a lot of time over the years at Tandoori Nights, one of my local Indian Restaurants (they are in Rustington and I highly recommend them to you!), getting to know the staff, being friendly and generally having a normal time. When Jemma and I got married we invited the staff to our big day and I was dead chuffed to see the manager, Mr Miah, and his family, turn up. I was intrigued too by the two huge presents he had under his arms. It was the first Christian meeting they'd ever been to and they thought it was wonderful. As a mark of their respect and friendship they bought us a barbecue and a microwave oven.

Then there's Angus, from the barber-shop, whom I've also got to know. During the summer of 1994, I was helping Gloria Hunniford present a series of Sunday morning TV shows, very imaginatively and creatively entitled, *Sunday*! They were all done via outside broadcast, and networked live across the UK. One Sunday, we were visiting Alnwick, Northumberland, and I had to interview a world champion sheep shearer. Things were fine in rehearsal, and I had memorised all of these fascinating facts about sheep, but when we went "live" to the nation, the poor guy just dried up. Knowing that I had a specific time to fill, and having used all my sheep questions up, I asked if he would actually let me have a go at shearing a sheep (I don't know who was more worried, the sheep or me!). While I was giving the sheep a haircut I just happened to mention, "My barber Angus would be proud of me."

Well, I don't think Angus would have been happier if I'd given him £1m in cash! He still talks about his TV mention to this day, and in all seriousness has worn out the video through showing it to so many people. He also asked me to officially open their new barbers shop. It was either Samantha Fox or me, so they opted for me, their friend. What a compliment!

Now, these two friends aren't saved yet, but they're both a little bit closer along the road - I know that for sure. But that's what friendship evangelism is all about, making friends and bringing people closer to Jesus.

Over the years I have been involved with a few pretty hare-brained network marketing schemes, selling everything from diet plans and ladies perfume, through to fizzy drinks machines. The name of the game was to sell the product and sell the business, so in theory you ended up with a team under you doing the same, making you money.

Some of the training principles and exercises were fascinating and are worth passing on for use in our friendship evangelism. One of the first jobs was to come up with a list of personal contacts in three main categories: biological, geographical and work.

1. Biological - as the name might suggest, our families
2. Geographical - people we know in our immediate area we have contact with, ie, milkman, postman, window-cleaner, the lads down the pub, other parents from school etc
3. Work - colleagues at work, school or university

So, in friendship evangelism I've found that it's helpful to identify our very own network of unbelievers, which we all have. Go on, put this book down now and make a list of your network from the above three categories. You should be able to get at least fifty different names without too much thought, and 100 if you think hard enough. I would wager that you actually know more unbelievers than you first thought. This list is a great place to start in making friends for God.

I hope I haven't left you feeling "got at" if you haven't got many, if any, friends who aren't Christians. It's easy once we're part of a church with so many different types of meetings, to end up without time to meet with non-Christians. The church I go to have a policy of only having two meetings a week - a Sunday and one in mid-week - to allow us the time to spend with non-Christian friends, practicing personal, friendship evangelism. To give you a helping hand, here's my top twenty tips on how to be a better friend:

1. Identify networks of unbelievers
2. Concentrate on building a small number of good friends
3. Pray for them
4. Think about what they might want from you
5. Think about what they might need from Jesus
6. Ask yourself how you can be a better friend to them
7. Do spend quality time with them
8. Listen to them
9. Don't just talk about yourself all the time
10. Be interested in them
11. Be interesting yourself
12. Trust them, and be honest with them about yourself
13. Be real - they'll probably see through any pretence anyway!
14. Share common interests

15. Invite people around to your home - the New Testament talks a lot about hospitality
16. Suggest you go out - pub, cinema, theatre, walk, swimming, etc
17. Be patient - friendships often take months and years to develop properly
18. Stay active not passive - keep in touch - don't always wait for them to call you
19. Be normal
20. Enjoy it

As a bit of a postscript to this chapter, I stopped writing a while ago and set off for Butlin's in Bognor Regis, where I perform for a few hours each week during the summer season. Following my own advice, I prayed for a "divine appointment" so that I could put some of these things into practice.

I arrived in Bognor and was performing some close-up magic around the tables when I accidentally cut my finger. Now this doesn't bode well for a professional performance, so after I'd finished entertaining I wandered into one of the manager's offices for a plaster. I got chatting with a manager called Chris, asking him questions about himself and being normal. I always try to find a "way in" - to try to find some common ground we can both relate to, and would you believe it, he was interested in magic.

Well, the upshot was that I spent over an hour chatting and laughing with him and have done ever since. We meet up at least once a week, and speak to each other even more regularly. Chris has become a good buddy of mine.

In Queen Victoria's time, a young woman had the good fortune of being escorted to dinner by William E. Gladstone, who was considered one of the most brilliant statesmen of the 19th century. On the following evening, the same young lady was escorted by Benjamin Disraeli, novelist, statesman and twice Prime Minister. When asked for her impression of these two great rivals, she replied: "After an evening with Gladstone, I thought he was the most brilliant man I'd ever met. After an evening with Disraeli, I thought myself to be the most fascinating woman in the world!"

So, it just goes to prove how important good, interesting friends are. Friendship evangelism really does work, and you have a lot of fun and laughs into the bargain. It's good for you and it's good for them - and that's a fact. Scientists have proved that fun and laughter are actually good for us. Laughter increases the amount of oxygen in the blood that helps the body to heal itself and resist further infection. It also lowers the heart rate, stimulates the appetite and burns up calories. A good laugh will also stimulate the body's natural painkilling tranquillisers, beta-endorphins, leading some experts to suggest that laughing can prevent ulcers and digestive disorders. So there you are: making friends and having a laugh is actually good for you and is easier than you think.

5: Praying for the Lost

The prayer meetings that began one evening in August 1727 in Herrnhut, Germany, helped change the shape of missionary endeavours for many years. They were started by Ludwig von Zinzendorf and lasted for over a century. During this time, more than 2,000 missionaries were sent in small teams all over the world.

In 1830, some 30,000 people were converted in Rochester, New York, while listening to the great evangelist Charles Finney. Finney took no credit for the mass conversions, and later said the reason for the success was that one man, who never actually attended the meetings: "gave himself to prayer".

In 1872, the American evangelist Dwight L. Moody began a major Gospel campaign in London, which God used to touch countless lives. Later Moody discovered that a "humble, bedridden girl had been praying".

In May 1934, a group of fervent Christian businessmen held a series of all-day prayer meetings in the pasture of a farm in Charlotte, USA. The group had held three similar meetings since they started praying together eighteen months earlier. Years later, the owner of the farm remembered a prayer that a man called Vernon Patterson had prayed that day: that out of Charlotte, North Carolina, the Lord would raise up someone to preach the Gospel to the ends of the earth. The farm's owner was Frank Graham, the father of Billy Graham.

More recently, in 1993, Paul Ariga, a key church leader from Japan, visited Argentina and received a special anointing for intercessory prayer. Upon his return to Japan, he recruited 13,000 fellow intercessors who collectively prayed for 350,000 hours for the lost in Japan. As a result,

125,000 people heard the Gospel and 22,000 became Christians.

During the global *March for Jesus* in London, on June 25 1994, some 75,000 people gathered in Hyde Park and took a few moments to pray for Bangladesh. They prayed for those in authority, the local and national government, for teachers, police and the military. In small groups, people prayed specifically for the salvation of the 116m people of one of the world's poorest nations, and the spreading of the Gospel. Together, the 75,000 proclaimed: "Lord, make your name great in Bangladesh! Let the people of Bangladesh be saved and come to a knowledge of the truth! Make your name great in Bangladesh". Some years later, missionaries in Bangladesh were asked if they'd noticed any changes in the country. They started to list a whole catalogue of incredible changes, and the date they could trace these changes to was June 25 1994.

In the northern part of the New Territories of Hong Kong, near the Chinese border, there were thirty-six churches until the early spring of 1996. Then, these churches started praying for revival. According to official government statistics, the crime rate in that area dropped by 40 per cent in the seven months since that time.

I appeared on a Christian television programme some years ago with Ed Silvoso, the founder of *Harvest Evangelism*, a missionary organisation committed to reaching entire cities for Jesus by implementing the essential principles of prayer evangelism. The "awakening" in Argentina received much of its impetus from the ministries of Omar and Marfa Cabrera from Buenos Aires, and also from Carlos Annacondia, whose evangelistic crusades beginning in the early 1980s resulted in many healing miracles and huge numbers of conversions in each of several cities. This included Mar del Plata, where 90,000 people came to Christ in 1984 during a six-week campaign.

We shouldn't really be too surprised by these wonderful stories, because we know that God can change things through prayer. If He can turn whole nations around He most certainly can do it with individuals. The Apostle James encourages us to continue praying: *"When a believing person prays, great things happen. Elijah was a human being just like us. He prayed that it would not rain, and it did not rain on the land for three and a half years! Then Elijah prayed again, the rain came down from the sky, and the land produced crops again"* (James 5:16-18). Now that is pretty powerful praying!

We sometimes get a bit confused about prayer. But, at the end of the day, prayer is simply about building a relationship with God. You get to know someone by being with them - it's the same with prayer, it's about spending time in the presence of God.

God loves to answer our prayers. *"Ask, and God will give to you. Search, and you will find. Knock, and the door will open for you. Yes, everyone who asks will receive. Everyone who searches will find. And everyone who knocks will have the door opened"*(Matthew 7:7-8). It's not about twisting God's arm, hoping that He gives us what we want. No, prayer is about relationship-building and discovering God's agenda, not ours.

It's important when we pray to focus our prayers. After all, if you've not got a target to aim at, you're never going to hit anything. It's often helpful to be detailed when we pray for specific individuals. John Allan, in his excellent book *Rescue Shop*, suggests using a Prayer Profile of specific information, to help focus our prayers. It could include:

1. Persons name
2. Age
3. Family
4. Interests and hobbies
5. Relationship with you
6. Opinion of Christianity
7. Most obvious needs
8. How you can help them
9. Qualities and failings
10. Fears and pressures

I'll tell you a personal story. Apologies if it sounds a bit flash or show-biz, but it's true; and it shows how keen God is to answer our prayers. As a young teenager growing up in the mid 1980s, my comedy heroes were people like Tommy Cooper, Morecambe and Wise, and Cannon and Ball. In particular, I used to love sitting down to watch *The Cannon and Ball Show* on TV on Saturday nights - they were real big stars. They enjoyed a massive eleven years of their own comedy series, starred in several Royal Variety Performances and were guests on all the major television shows. Their feature film, *The Boys in Blue*, in addition to its cinema success, went on to become a video best seller. The boys were also the subject of *This Is Your Life*. On stage, they broke records in theatres all over the UK and in 1981 played a six-week run at London's *Dominion Theatre*, in which every seat was sold before opening night. Their 1988 pantomime at the world famous *London Palladium* broke all previous box office records, and they created the record for the largest box office amount taken in one week in British theatre history.

Huge success brought many problems and difficulties though. In Bobby Ball's autobiography *My Life*, he explained how his ego, and his love of women, alcohol and fighting made him an impossible person to work with. His career was on the way up, but his private life was on the way down, until in 1986 he met Jesus.

I was amazed that one of my heroes has got saved, well that got me praying for Tommy Cannon in a big way - I really went to town on it, as I know many other Christians did too. Tommy had a similar story to tell, and every area of his life suffered because of their huge success, including his marriage. Imagine Tommy's surprise when suddenly everything about Bobby changed. He started talking about his family, started treating other people with respect, and eventually told Tommy that he had become a Christian. Tommy's immediate reaction was that his mate had become a religious nutcase! Eventually though, since the change in Bobby was genuine, deep and possibly a miracle, Tommy was intrigued to know more. Surprise, surprise, Tommy became a Christian some eight years later. What an answer to prayer!

But God hadn't finished. In 1995, I was invited to join Bobby and Tommy on the *The Cannon and Ball Gospel Show*, playing to huge audiences across the length and breadth of the UK. Here I was on stage with the boys, the very same blokes that I had prayed would find Jesus, now performing and talking about our faith together. Now that's what I call a major answer to prayer.

Prayer should be key in all our evangelistic endeavours. Let me give you a prayer check-list to get you praying more effectively:

1. Be specific - specific prayers get specific answers
2. Pray with others - it helps to keep the discipline going
3. Pray for boldness - God is the source of power, so ask Him for more (Acts 4:29)
4. Pray for the workers - your prayers could make all the difference (1 Thessalonians 5:25)
5. Pray for more workers - we need to see more people doing evangelism (Luke 10:2)
6. Don't give up - keep going, don't just pray when you feel like it (1 Thessalonians 5:17)
7. Pray with faith - believe for the impossible (Ephesians 3:20)
8. Pray for compassion - ask God to give you more compassion for the lost

9. Pray for open doors - that God will give you, and you will notice these opportunities (Colossians 4:3)
10. Pray for revival - not just good meetings, but a sovereign move of God (Hosea 10:12)

"I would rather teach one man to pray than ten men to preach."
(Charles Spurgeon)

"The man who mobilises the Christian church to pray will make the greatest contribution to world evangelisation in history."
(Andrew Murray)

6: What Is This Good News?

There I was, minding my own business, out shopping on a Saturday afternoon. Out of the corner of my eye I noticed an earnest looking chap, shouting about the Bible. He had a line of six other gentlemen behind him, all clutching small Bibles, and then a row of ladies wearing head scarves behind them. I stood and watched and listened to the doom and gloom they were communicating. After they finished their "presentation", to which, I might add, no-one was playing a blind bit of notice, I just had to go and say something. I explained that I was a Christian from a local Church, and that I had some experience in street work, and made some subtle suggestions in terms of presentation and communicating fun and life and generally being good news. This chap turned to me, looked at my colourful Swatch wrist-watch and said: "Well, you can't be a Christian anyway with a watch like that". With that, they marched off home. I just couldn't believe it! Certainly not very good news.

Many people I meet think that to be a Christian you need to wear a tight fitting tank top, grey slacks, a pair of ankle-length socks underneath sandals, go to church twenty-five times on a Sunday, watch *Songs of Praise*, go to Israel on holiday, and have a beard - and that's just the women!

Others have a preconceived view of God. They see Him as some sort of Father Christmas look-alike, floating around on a white cloud and wearing flowing robes, while strumming away on a gold harp. Jesus is seen by many as a 1st century religious hippie who travelled with twelve friends, doing wimpy things like kissing babies and telling people off for laughing! A bit of an exaggeration perhaps ... perhaps not.

Let's look at the word evangelism, or "Evangel". Evangel literally

means Good News. But what is this Good News and how do we effectively tell others who don't know what it is? Please don't try to get a
migraine figuring it out, I'll try to explain later on.

I use the word "try" because even the Bible doesn't give us an easy
answer. The Bible doesn't even use the word evangelism, nor does the
word evangelist (the Greek word, "Euangelistes") occur often in the
Bible. Only three times in fact: Philip who was called an evangelist (Acts
21:8), Timothy was told to *"do the work of an evangelist"* (2 Timothy
4:5) and Paul describes the evangelist as one of the gifts Jesus has given
to the Church (Ephesians 4:11).

Having said all of that, the verb form of the word, "euangelizo", appears
a lot of times, fifty-two times to be precise, and simply put it means "to pro-
claim the Good News". The angels did it when they told people about Jesus'
birth (Luke 2:10) and Jesus proclaimed the evangel of the Kingdom (Mark
1:14) - I could give you a further fifty examples. By using verbs (doing
words) to talk about evangelism, the Bible couldn't really make it more obvious that evangelism is about action - actually doing it.

But how do we get on with it, and what do we actually say? Some see
evangelism as a certain magic technique or your money back, or associ-
ate it with high pressure salesmanship. They find it very unnatural. I guar-
antee you that it doesn't have to be that way. Paul puts it this way: *"God
... through Christ changed us from enemies into his friends and gave us
the task of making others his friends also"* (2 Corinthians 5:18).

Dr James Engel, formerly a marketing professor at Ohio State
University, developed a scale while looking at the process of evangelism.
Engel's scale shows at a glance how far along the road a person is to
knowing Jesus and becoming a disciple. Now I know what you're thinking: God is God and He doesn't have to work to scale's or diagrams and
can intervene in amazing supernatural ways. Absolutely true. But this
scale is probably a helpful way in seeing how the Good News can work.
The stages Engel's suggests are as follows:

-8	Awareness of Supreme Being
-7	Initial awareness of the Gospel
-6	Awareness of fundamentals of the Gospel
-5	A grasp of the implications of the Gospel
-4	Positive attitude towards the Gospel
-3	A recognition of personal problems
-2	Decision to do something about it
-1	Repentance and new faith in Jesus

NEW CREATION
+1   Evaluation of decision
+2   Integrated into the Church
+3   Conceptual and behavioural growth
+4   Communion with God
+5   Active in evangelism

I bet you never realised evangelism and the Gospel were so technical! The actual heart of the Gospel - the Greek word "kerygma" - is found throughout the New Testament, but different emphasis is put on it each time, with bits added or taken away depending on the situation, and who was communicating to whom. There is one very famous verse, worn on T-shirts, seen on car stickers and also often seen in key positions during major sporting occasions, that sums the whole thing up: *"God loved the world so much that he gave his one and only Son so that whoever believes in him may not be lost, but have eternal life"* (John 3:16).

So here is the Gospel, the best news ever. What a wonderful verse. It starts with God's love, His wonderful love, in sending his Son, His *"one and only son"*, as the *Youth Bible* puts it. We are so special to Him that He *gave* Jesus, knowing full well He would suffer and die for us. The Jews wrongly believed that the Messiah would be coming just for them, to their nation. But Jesus tells us that He came for the whole world, Jews and Gentiles alike, so anyone who believes won't die, for God has taken away our sin and we're now entitled to eternal life. Fantastic isn't it?

Over the years, I have had the very great privilege of travelling far and wide with the wonderful message, in school and colleges, on the radio, in night clubs and once even a packed Canterbury Cathedral. I could tell you story after story about how God has changed lives, as people, young and old, have heard this message of the Gospel. I could tell you about the barbecue I spoke at, where international students from Japan, Brazil, Peru, Switzerland, Hungary, Poland, Germany, Grand Canaria, Latvia and Slovakia heard the Gospel, many of them for the first time. Or the time seventy teenagers got saved at an end of week schools concert in West Sussex; or the eighty-four men, women, boys and girls in Southampton; or the twenty-three young people in Luzern, Switzerland who heard about Jesus and wanted to become Christians; I could go on and on!

Did I tell you about my trip to Wokingham where I spoke at an Anglican church and twenty people made commitments, including the organiser? Or the time a father and son made independent commitments at a church in Littlehampton that they happened to be visiting for the first time? Or about one of the smallest events I've ever spoken at, in Lymington, where all six of the unbelievers made first-time commitments? Then there was the occasion in Northern Ireland when I spent an hour, yes I did say an hour, on *Cool FM* radio's drive time show (the equivalent of *BBC Radio 2*), talking about escapology, show business and Jesus - it was quite amazing! I could go on and on and on ...

I became a Christian during my teenage years and was desperate to share my faith. But no-one really told me how to go about it: what I had to say, what not to say etc, etc, so I'm going to let you into some techniques that I personally use and find effective. I hold no claims to inventing them, and I know there are strengths and weakensses with techniques, but sometimes when you've only got two minutes in a crowded lift to explain the Gospel, it helps to know what you want to say, clearly and concisely.

"Be wise in the way you act with people who are not believers, making the most of every opportunity" (Colossians 4:5).

7: Knowing What To Say

Nicodemus, an important Jewish ruler and teacher, came to Jesus with a stack of questions. But most of them weren't really relevant to his conversation with Jesus. You will notice that Jesus refused to be sidetracked and got straight to what He wanted to say, using language and illustrations that Nicodemus would understand.

In our conversations, we need to be the same. We need to be focused on what we want to say. Now, it's unlikely we'll ever have the time to go right through the entire Bible with someone, so we need to select the important facts that people need to know and understand if they want to become Christians.

Here it is then, the Gospel in a "nutshell": God planned a great relationship with people, but people rebelled against God and this sin resulted in separation from God. Jesus made the way back to God through His life, death and resurrection, so that if we put our faith in Him we will receive forgiveness and have our original relationship with God restored.

In my mind, it's even simpler. I'm always thinking those four key words: God, Sin, Jesus and Faith. But it's not enough to just reel off a nice story. We need to back it up with verses from the Bible, and it's handy to have some illustrations that people can relate to. Here are some great verses, and some of my favourite stories and illustrations to back up these four main facts:

GOD

"So God created human beings in his image" (Genesis 1:27).

"Examine and see how good the Lord is. Happy is the person who trusts in him" (Psalm 34:8).

"God began by making one person, and from him came all the different people who live everywhere in the world. God wanted them to look for him and perhaps search all around for him and find him, though he is not far from any of us" (Acts 17:26-27).

"Through his power all things were made - things in heaven and on earth, things seen and unseen, all powers, authorities, lords and rulers" (Colossians 1:16).

Some might say you can't believe what you can't see with your own eyes. But there's a whole stack of things we believe in that we can't physically see with our own eyes. What about electricity? You can't actually see it, but you can see the effects of electricity: when you flick a switch a light comes on. In the same way, although you can't see God, you can see the effects of God. Human beings need oxygen to breathe and we get this oxygen from plants. The plants, however, need carbon dioxide to survive: no prizes for guessing who gives them that. Yes, it's humans - what a nice arrangement!

People who say there's no God are like a six-year-old child saying there is no such thing as passionate love - they just haven't experienced it.

SIN

"We all have wandered away like sheep; each of us has gone his own way. But the Lord has put on him the punishment for all the evil we have done" (Isaiah 53:6).

"I will forgive them for the wicked things they did, and I will not remember their sins any more" (Jeremiah 31:34).

"There is no God like you. You forgive those who are guilty of sin; you don't look at the sins of your people who are left alive. You will not stay angry for ever, because you enjoy being kind" (Micah 7:18-19).

"From that time Jesus began to preach, saying, 'Change your hearts and lives, because the kingdom of heaven is near'" (Matthew 4:17).

"So you must change your hearts and lives! Come back to God, and he will forgive your sins" (Acts 3:19).

"All have sinned and are not good enough for God's glory" (Romans 3:23).

"But if we confess our sins, he will forgive our sins, because we can trust God to do what is right. He will cleanse us from all the wrongs we have done" (1 John 1:9).

A famous Rabbi was walking with some of his disciples when one of them asked, "Rabbi, when should a man stop sinning and repent?" The Rabbi calmly replied, "You should be sure to repent on the last day of your life." "But," protested several of his disciples, "we can never be sure which day will be the last day of our life." The famous Rabbi smiled and said, "The answer to that problem is very simple. Repent now."

When God buries our sins in the deepest sea, He posts a sign that reads: "No Fishing"!

Originally the word "sin" was the word archers used to describe missing the target. In the same way, we've all missed the target God planned for us.

JESUS

"God loved the world so much that he gave his one and only Son so that whoever believes in him may not be lost, but have eternal life" (John 3:16).

"A thief comes to steal and kill and destroy, but I come to give life - life in all its fullness" (John 10:10).

"But God shows his great love for us in this way: Christ died for us while we were still sinners." (Romans 5:8).

"God was pleased for all of himself to live in Christ. And through Christ, God has brought all things back to himself again - things on earth and things in heaven. God made peace through the blood of Christ's death on the cross" (Colossians 1:19-20).

"He saved us because of his mercy. It was not because of good deeds we did to be right with him. He saved us through the washing that made us new people through the Holy Spirit" (Titus 3: 5-7).

"Christ himself suffered for sins once. He was not guilty, but he suffered for those who are guilty to bring you to God. His body was killed, but he was made alive in the spirit" (1 Peter 3:18).

A wealthy English family once invited friends to spend some time with them at their beautiful estate. The happy gathering was almost plunged into a terrible tragedy on the first day. The children were swimming and one of them got into deep water and was drowning. Fortunately, the gardener heard the screams and plunged into the pool to rescue the helpless victim. The young child was Winston Churchill. His parents, deeply grateful to the gardener, asked what they could do to reward him. He hesitated, then said, "I wish my son could go to college someday and become a doctor." "We'll pay his way," replied Churchill's parents.

Years later, while Sir Winston was Prime Minister, he was stricken with pneumonia. Greatly concerned, the King summoned the best physician who could be found to the bedside of the ailing leader. That doctor was Sir Alexander Fleming, the man who invented penicillin. Fleming was also the son of the gardener who had saved Winston from drowning all those years before! Later, Churchill said, "Rarely, has one man owed his life twice to the same person."

According to an ancient Oriental tradition, whenever a debt was settled, either by payment or forgiveness, the creditor would take the cancelled bond and nail it over the door of the one who owed it. Anyone passing could then see that it had been paid in full.

FAITH

"Trust the Lord with all your heart, and don't depend on your own understanding" (Proverbs 3:5).

"You, Lord, give true peace to those who depend on you, because they trust you. So, trust the Lord always because his is our Rock for ever" (Isaiah 26:3-4).

"If you use your mouth to say, "Jesus is Lord", and if you believe in your heart that God raised Jesus from the dead, you will be saved" (Romans 10:9).

"You have been saved by grace through believing. You did not save

yourselves: it was a gift from God. It was not the result of your own work, so you cannot boast about it" (Ephesians 2:8-9).

Yesterday I jumped on a plane and flew to appear on a TV programme. I was strung 10 feet high, upside down, in a studio and escaped from a strait jacket in under one minute. Maybe not your average sort of day, I know. But I put my life in other people's hands at least twice in that 24-hours. I didn't ask to see the pilot's licence to check that he was adequately trained and, when I got to the studio, I didn't ask to see Nick, the studio technician's credentials either. I trusted that his equipment would keep me safe, so that I wouldn't end up falling on my head.

When my wife, Jemma, makes me a cup of coffee, I drink it without question. I don't examine it, or test the chemicals to make sure she's not trying to bump me off for the insurance money! No, I trust her, and that's what faith is all about - trust. Some may say that Christianity is "blind faith". But that's not so. However, with Jesus, you have to take your first steps towards Him before you can be really sure He's there.

When John Patton was translating the Bible for a South Seas Island tribe, he discovered that they had no word for trust or faith. One day a native, who had been running hard, came into the missionary's house, crashed out in a large chair and said: "It's good to rest my whole weight on this chair." That's it, thought Patton, I'll translate faith as "resting one's whole weight on God".

8: Other Ways

Good communication is an important thing. It is very easy for people to get the "wrong end of the stick" if we're not very clear about what we're trying to say. And on a few occasions, a mistake is corrected by an even greater mistake. The following comedy of errors actually occurred in an American newspaper several years ago.

First Day: FOR SALE - R. D. Jones has one sewing machine for sale. Phone 958 3030 after 7.00pm and ask for Mrs Kelly who lives with him cheap.

The next day the advertisement was corrected to read: NOTICE - We regret having erred in R. D. Jones's ad yesterday. It should have read: One sewing machine for sale. Cheap. Phone 958 3030 and ask for Mrs Kelly who lives with him after 7.00pm.

The second correction was corrected the day after. It read: R. D. Jones has informed us that he has received several anonymous telephone calls because of the error we made in his classified advertisement yesterday. His advertisement stands corrected as follows: FOR SALE - R. D. Jones has one sewing machine for sale. Cheap. Phone 958 3030 after 7.00pm and ask for Mrs Kelly who loves with him.

Finally, the day after, Mr Jones corrected the advertisement himself with a second advertisement:

NOTICE - I, R. D. Jones, have no sewing machine for sale. I SMASHED IT. Don't call 958 3030 as the telephone has been taken out. I have not been carrying on with Mrs Kelly. Until yesterday she was my housekeeper, but SHE QUIT!

A bit far-fetched perhaps, but I'm told it really did happen. Good communication is so important. I hope you've been finding some of the techniques I've been explaining helpful. Another one follows here, but first let me say this: any communication that persuades people to come to Jesus isn't just down to us. Witnessing isn't selling double glazing by clever sales techniques, neither is it brainwashing or beating people over the head with a big black Bible until they say "yes". Of course God uses us as human communicators, which is brilliant, but it is ultimately He who does the real work. We can explain the Good News and answer all their tough questions, we can tell them that they have sinned and done wrong, but it's the Holy Spirit that actually convicts them of their sin. *"When the Helper comes, he will prove to the people of the world the truth about sin, about being right with God and about judgement"* (John 16:8).

I hope that's clear. We can save no-one without God, and most of the time He can save no-one without us being available to communicate his message. Quite simply, we need Him, and He needs us - what a privilege. On we go then, with a couple of excellent ways of explaining the Good News by taking you through the Bible.

I particularly like these methods when I'm working outside the UK. I don't have much of a flair for languages - in fact during a time in Paris, in my eagerness to introduce myself as an Escape Artist in French, I ended up calling myself an "Escaping Peeping Tom" - so I have a collection of foreign Bibles, and I point my way through!

Probably the most famous version is one known as the *Roman Road*, which systematically takes you through the book of "Romans". The original version starts with "sin", which I don't think is a terrible positive place to start. Instead I do it beginning with God's creative love - hope you don't mind!

THE ROMAN ROAD

"There are things about Him that people cannot see - his eternal power and all things that make him God. But since the beginning of the world these things have been easy to understand by what God has made. So people have no excuse for the bad things that they do" (Romans 1:20).

"All have sinned and are not good enough for God's glory" (Romans 3:23).

"When people sin, they earn what sin pays - death. But God gives us a free gift - life for ever in Christ Jesus our Lord"(Romans 6:23).

"So now, those who are in Christ Jesus are not judged guilty" (Romans 8:1).

"We believe with our hearts, and so we are made right with God. And we use our mouths to say that we believe, and so we are saved" (Romans 10:9).

"So brothers and sisters, since God has shown us great mercy, I beg you to offer your lives as a living sacrifice to him. Your offering must be only for God and pleasing to him, which is the spiritual way for you to worship. Do not change yourselves to be like the people of this world, but be changed within by a new way of thinking. Then you will be able to decide what God wants for you; you will know what is good and pleasing to him and what is perfect" (Romans 12:1-2).

It's a great method, I'm sure you'll agree. But you might be put off by the fact that you've got a memory likc a sieve, and will never remember the six different verses. Don't worry, help is at hand. Why not just remember the first one, Romans 1:20, and then in the margin of your Bible when you turn to it, have the next verse, Romans 3:23 written down, and so on. Clever isn't it? Why not give it a go?

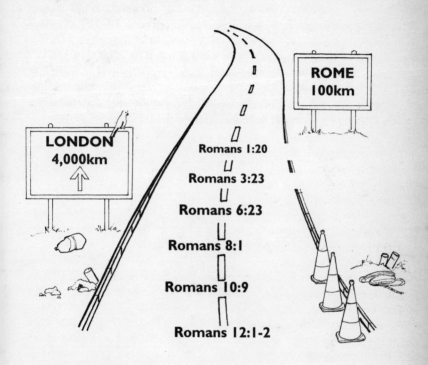

Romans 1:20

Romans 3:23

Romans 6:23

Romans 8:1

Romans 10:9

Romans 12:1-2

ANOTHER METHOD

Here's another way of explaining the Gospel, using verses from the New Testament. It starts with Romans and uses other books too. Try it yourself.

"All have sinned and are not good enough for God's glory" (Romans 3:23).

"When people sin, they earn what sin pays - death. But God gives us a free gift - life for ever in Christ Jesus our Lord" (Romans 6:23).

"Just as everyone must die once and be judged, so Christ was offered as a sacrifice once to take away the sins of many people" (Hebrews 9:27-28).

"But God shows his great love for us in this way: Christ died for us while we were still sinners" (Romans 5:8).

"I mean that you have been saved by grace through believing. You did not save yourselves: it was a gift from God. It was not the result of your own work, so you cannot boast about it" (Ephesians 2:8-9).

"If you ask me for anything in my name, I will do it" (John 14:14).

"This is what God told us: God has given us eternal life, and this life is in his Son. Whoever has the Son has life, but whoever does not have the Son of God does not have life" (1 John 5:11-12).

9: Using Your Story

I have to admit to being a bit of a telly addict. I avidly watch cookery programmes, quizzes and all the "soaps", but most of all love chat shows, because I'm interested in other people's lives. Put another way, I'm a bit nosey and enjoy finding out what others have been and are currently doing! I guess most of us can relate to that. The huge range of high street glossy magazines that are sold and read just reinforce the point that we find other people's lives and stories just plain fascinating.

For example, John Wesley's personal story has always made a profound impact on all who have read it. Here is a summary of how he came to Jesus.

Wesley went to Oxford Seminary and then became a minister in the Church of England, where he served for about ten years. Towards the end of this time, in approximately 1735, he became a missionary from England to Georgia, USA. All of his life he had been quite a failure in his ministry, though he was very pious. He got up at 4.00am and prayed for two hours. He would then read the Bible for an hour before going to the jails, prisons and hospitals to minister to all manner of people. He would teach, pray for, and help others until late at night. He did this for years. In fact, the Methodist Church gets its name from the methodical life of piety that Wesley and his friends lived.

On his way home from America, there was a great storm at sea. The little ship in which they were sailing was about to sink. Huge waves broke over the ship and the wind roared in the sails. Wesley feared he was going to die that night and he was terrified. He had no assurance of what would happen to him when he died. Despite all his efforts to be good, death now for him was just a big black question mark. On one side of the ship was a group of men who were singing hymns. He asked them: "How can you sing when this very night you are going to die?" They replied: "If this ship goes down we will go up to be with the Lord forever." Wesley went away shaking his head, thinking to himself: "How can they know that? What have they done that I have not done?" Then he thought: "I came to America to convert the heathen, but who shall convert me?"

They survived the storm and eventually the ship made it back to England. Wesley went to London and found his way to Aldersgate Street and a small chapel. There he heard a man reading a sermon that had been written two centuries before by Martin Luther, entitled: *Luther's Preface to the Book of Romans*. This sermon described what real faith was. It is trusting in Jesus for salvation and not relying on our good works. Wesley suddenly realised that he had been on the "wrong road" all his life. That night he wrote these words in his journal: "About a quarter before nine, while he was describing the change which God works in the heart through faith in Christ, I felt my heart strangely warmed. I felt I did not trust in Christ, Christ alone, for salvation, and an assurance was given me that he had taken away my sins, even mine, and saved me from the law of sin and death."

Following his dramatic conversion, John Wesley, founder of the Methodist Church, spent fifty-two years of his life riding around Britain on horseback preaching the Gospel. He got up each morning at 4.00am and covered 225,000 miles, and preached 40,000 sermons. He said of his remarkable life and ministry: "I look upon all the world as my parish ... in whatever part of it I am, I judge it right to declare unto all that are willing to hear the glad tiding of salvation".

In the same way, the early Christians didn't just tell others about Jesus' story, they also told their own stories. Paul explained how he met with Jesus on the road to Damascus at least twice (Acts 22 and Acts 26). Peter and John did it as well: *"We cannot keep quiet. We must speak about what we have seen and heard"* (Acts 4:20). They knew that their personal experience could not be dismissed; it was a powerful witnessing tool. The book of Acts tells us that the Jewish leaders *"were amazed"* by their words (Acts 4:13), because they knew that Peter and Simon had no special training or education. They realised they both *"had been with Jesus"* (Acts 4:13).

The problem many Christians have with sharing, or should I say not sharing, their testimony is that they think it is just too normal. By the way, I really don't like using the word "testimony". For me it smacks of religious jargon, words that doesn't really mean much to your average "unsaved" person. When football fans hear the word "testimony" they will automatically think of a "testimonial" game, held in honour of long and loyal service from a player. Others might think the word means some sort of solemn statement under oath in court. Very few will realise that you are giving them an enrapturing account of how you met Jesus! As a teenager, stories of vicious gang leaders, violent Hell's Angels and evil satanists turning to Jesus thrilled me, but left me feeling rather inadequate. They made me feel that my story was insignificant and just plain ordinary. But then someone explained that I would be able to relate and identify far more with the average person because I didn't have such a spectacular story to tell - and that's absolutely true.

What we need to do is to make our personal story more effective. Let's start by looking at Paul in Acts 22:1-21, and see how he used his story in a very effective way, as he explained what life was like before knowing Jesus, how he came to meet Him, and what happened afterwards:

BEFORE

"Paul said, 'Friends, fellow Jews, listen to my defence to you.' When the Jews heard him speaking the Jewish language, they became very quiet. Paul said, "I am a Jew, born in Tarsus in the country of Cilicia, but I grew up in this city. I was a student of Gamaliel, who carefully taught me everything about the law of our ancestors. I was very serious about serving God, just as are all of you here today. I persecuted the people who followed the Way of Jesus, and some of them were even killed. I arrested men and women and put them in jail. The high priest and the whole council of elders Jewish can tell you this is true. They gave me letters to the Jewish brothers in Damascus. So I was going there to arrest these people and bring them back to Jerusalem to be punished" (Acts 22:1-5).

You need to tell it "how it is". It is often such a temptation, particularly if we have a very ordinary story, to exaggerate our past lives a little bit, just to make the story more exciting. Not a good idea! We need to be honest and straight down the line with people. Explain, like Paul did, what you were like, where you are from, what life was like, your thoughts and attitudes before you became a Christian. Don't bore your listener with boring, incidentals though!

DURING

"At about noon when I came near Damascus a bright light from heaven suddenly flashed all around me. I fell to the ground and heard a

voice saying, 'Saul, Saul, why are you persecuting me?' I asked, 'Who are you, Lord?' The voice said, 'I am Jesus from Nazareth whom you are persecuting.' Those who were with me did not hear the voice, but they saw the light. I said, 'What shall I do, Lord?' The Lord answered, 'Get up and go to Damascus. There you will be told about all the things I have planned for you to do.' I could not see, because the bright light had made me blind. So my companions led me into Damascus.

"There a man named Ananias came to me. He was a religious man; he obeyed the law of Moses, and all the Jews who lived there respected him. He stood by me and said, 'Brother Saul, see again!' Immediately I was able to see him. He said, 'The God of our ancestors chose you long ago to know his plan, to see the Righteous One and to hear words from him. You will be his witness to all people, telling them about what you have seen and heard. Now, why wait any longer? Get up, be baptised and wash your sins away, trusting in him to save you'" (Acts 22:6-16).

Explain how you came to realise you had a need for Jesus in your life and how you actually came to become a Christian. Unbelievers find this part fascinating, they really do. Recount how you were feeling at the moment of your decision and give lots of personal details. Remember to use language that they can relate to. Words like "saved", "blessed" and "washed in the blood" are most definitely out!

AFTER

"Later, when I returned to Jerusalem, I was praying in the Temple, and I saw a vision. I saw the Lord saying to me, 'Hurry! Leave Jerusalem now! The people here will not accept the truth about me.' But I said, 'Lord, they know that in every synagogue I put the believers in jail and beat them. They also know I was there when Stephen, your witness, was killed. I stood there agreeing and holding the coats of those who were killing him!' But the Lord said to me, 'Leave now. I will send you far away to the non-Jewish people'" (Acts 22:17-21).

Don't be dishonest about this either. It's a fact that when people become Christians their problems don't disappear overnight. So please be honest - we don't want to "con" people into the Kingdom of God. Do, however explain how being a Christian has helped with your problems, and what knowing Jesus means in your life today.

Don't just use old illustrations though. Make your story really up-to-date. Be ready to change this part of your story every week, if not every day.

Most importantly, at the end of your story, don't just leave it at that. Why not ask: "what do you think about having a personal relationship with Jesus yourself?" This could well be the time for someone to want it for themselves. So go and tell your story, and tell it like it is.

10: Questions, Questions

As I've already mentioned, one of the reasons Christians often don't share their faith, is that they're worried that unbelievers will ask them tough questions about Christianity that they just won't be able to answer.

Good news and bad news on this one. The bad news is that people do tend to ask rather tricky questions, but the good news they do tend to be the same ones; what I affectionately call "The Dirty Dozen".

1. Who made God?
2 How can you believe in something you can't see?
3. What about creation?
4. Hasn't science disproved it all?
5. Surely you can't believe the Bible?
6. Did Jesus really exist?
7. Did Jesus really come back to life?
8. What about suffering?
9. Do miracles still happen?
10. Isn't it all in the mind?
11. What about the other religions?
12. Won't a good life do?

Knowing these questions means that we can try to come up with some answers. It's not enough to just come up with some clever, glib answers. No-one likes a "know it all". Instead, let's keep our answers simple, packed full of personal experience (no-one can argue with that), with Bible references and illustrations that will be understood, and always try to refocus the conversation back onto Jesus.

So here we go: twelve short, and certainly not exhaustive, answers to the most common questions I get asked.

WHO MADE GOD?

No-one! He's always been there and always will be. Now that's a bit hard for our tiny minds to understand. After all, everything needs to be created. Yes, that's true for physical things, like the keyboard I'm thumping away at to write this book, or the chair I'm currently sitting on, but the Bible says God isn't "physical", but instead, "spiritual". So it's not too illogical to suggest that spiritual things don't have to obey physical laws, and in fact exist totally outside of these laws.

It's a strange thing, isn't it? The whole concept of things existing outside of time and space was virtually dismissed until Albert Einstein came along with his theory of relativity. I know this is all so hard to get our heads around, but these facts do make it a little easier to understand the Bible's teaching about God existing outside time and space, as we know it.

"To you, a thousand years is like the passing of a day, or like a few hours in the night" (Psalm 90:4).

"He was there before anything was made, and all things continue because of him" (Colossians 1:17).

"Jesus Christ is the same yesterday, today and for ever" (Hebrews 13:8).

"But do not forget this one thing, dear friends; to the Lord one day is as a thousand years, and a thousand years is as one day" (2 Peter 3:8).

Eugene Crenan, one of the astronauts who enjoyed the exciting experience of walking on the moon, said with wonder as he looked at our planet from space: "Our world appears big and beautiful, all blue and white! You can see from the Antarctic to the North Pole. The earth looks so perfect. There are no strings to hold it up; there is no fulcrum upon which it rests." Contemplating the infinity of space and time, he said he felt as if he were seeing the earth from God's perspective.

HOW CAN YOU BELIEVE IN SOMETHING YOU CAN'T SEE?

Of course it's true that you can't see God. Or for that matter, taste, touch or smell Him. But so what? Sometimes you just have to believe in things that you can't see. I've already mentioned electricity; then there's radio waves - you just know when you turn on your radio that sound is going to come out. What about microwaves? You can't see those either, but I know full well that when I put my half-eaten, cold chicken vindaloo into the microwave to heat up, four minutes later it's piping hot (and absolutely delicious!).

We can see the effects of God all around us in the wonders of creation, and in our lives, we can see how God has changed us as He has met with us and impacted our lives for good. This is a great time to share your personal experience of how you became a Christian and what knowing God has done for you.

Jim Bishop's article, which follows here, puts the whole thing into perspective:

There is no God. All of the wonders around us are accidental. No almighty hand made a thousand stars. They made themselves. No power keeps them on their steady course. The earth spins itself to keep the oceans from falling off towards the sun. Infants teach themselves to cry when they are hungry or hurt. A small flower invented itself so that we could extract digitalis for sick hearts.

The earth gave itself day and night, tilted itself so that we get seasons. Without the magnetic poles man would be unable to navigate the trackless oceans of water and air, but they just grew there.

How about the sugar thermostat in the pancreas? It maintains a level of sugar in the blood sufficient for energy. Without it, all of us would fall into a coma and die.

Why does snow sit on mountain-tops waiting for the warm spring sun to melt it at just the right time for the young crops in farms below to drink? A very lovely accident.

The human heart will beat for seventy to eighty years or more without faltering. How does it get sufficient rest between beats? A kidney will filter poison from the blood, and leave good things alone. How does it know one from the other?

Who gave the human tongue flexibility to form words, and a brain to understand them, but denied it to the animals?

Who showed a womb how to take the love of two persons and keep

splitting a tiny ovum until, in time, a baby would have the proper number of fingers, eyes and ears and hair in the right places, and come into
the world when it is strong enough to sustain life?

There is no God?

WHAT ABOUT CREATION?

Never forget that the Theory of Evolution is just that - a theory.
Indeed, it is less of a scientific theory and more of a philosophy about the
origins of life and the meaning of mankind. As such it is clearly contra-
dictory to the Bible's account of creation.

But this theory isn't just at odds with the Bible, it also contradicts
some very basic laws of science. Scientists tell us about the second law of
thermodynamics, a law of physics, which simply tells us that left to itself,
everything tends to become less ordered, not more ordered or "complex".
It's pretty obvious really, even to a non-scientific person like me: things
grow old, run down, decay and eventually die. Batteries run out, your
clothes get worn and faded, things break - ultimately, everything falls
apart - things do not get more complex, as evolution would suggest.

Always remember: evolution is not a fact. We are often under the
impression that Christians are the only one's who don't believe in evolution. The good news, however, is that dozens of reputable scientists don't
either! Professor Wickramasinghe, the astronomer, said this: "The idea
that life was put together by random shuffling of constituent molecules
can be shown to be as ridiculous and improbable as the proposition that a
tornado blowing through a junk yard may assemble a Boeing 747. The
aircraft had a creator and so might life." Even Charles Darwin subscribed
to a missionary society and held evangelistic meetings in his garden.

Surely, if God is God, then He would have no problem in creating the
world exactly as is written in Genesis chapter's 1-3. Having said that,
while some Christians believe He created the world in six literal days,
others would suggest that the days weren't actual 24-hour days as we
know them today. The sun wasn't recorded as being created until the
fourth day, so perhaps those first three days weren't solar (24 hour) days
after all.

Many years ago, the famous scientist Sir Isaac Newton, had an exact
replica of the solar system made in miniature. At its centre was a large gold-
en ball representing the sun, and revolving around it were small spheres
attached at the ends by rods of varying lengths. They represented Mercury,
Venus, Earth, Mars and the other planets. These were all geared together by
cogs and belts to make them move around the sun in perfect harmony.

One day, as Newton was studying the model, a friend who did not believe in the Biblical account of creation, stopped by for a visit. Marvelling at the device and watching as the scientist made the heavenly bodies move on their own orbits, the man exclaimed: "My, Newton, what an exquisite thing! Who made it for you?" Without even looking up, Sir Isaac replied: "Nobody." "Nobody?" replied his friend, puzzled. "That's right! I said nobody! All of these balls, cogs, belts and gears just happened to come together, and wonder of wonders, by chance they began revolving in their set orbits with perfect timing."

His friend soon got the message! It was plain stupid to suppose that the model merely happened. But it was even more stupid to accept the theory that the earth and the vast universe came into being by just chance. Isn't it more logical to believe what the Bible says: *"In the beginning, God created the sky and the earth"* (Genesis 1:1).

HASN'T SCIENCE DISPROVED IT ALL?

It is scientifically impossible to prove the existence of God, though, I might add, it is scientifically impossible to disprove it too. You just can't put God in a test tube and analyse Him. So sorry, there isn't any concrete proof that tells us that God lives.

Having said that, the Bible tells us that He exists. Christians believe that the Bible is more than just a book - that in fact it is the actual Word of God.

We also know that God exists because He has appeared to us. Jesus was God wrapped up in human form: *"The Word became human and lived amongst us"* (John 1:14). The author goes on to tell us that: *"... he [Jesus] has shown us what God is like"* (John 1:18).

We can look at our wonderful world: human beings, animals, trees and the weather. Surely it couldn't have happened by accident. Our world bears all the hallmarks of a Creator. The human body, for example, is a masterpiece of incredible design. Beautifully engineered, it is governed by several hundred systems of control - each interacting with and affecting the other. The brain has 10 billion nerve cells to record what a person sees and hears. The skin has more than 2m tiny sweat glands - about 3,000 per square inch, all part of the intricate system that keeps the body at an even temperature. A "pump" in the chest makes the blood travel 168m miles a day - that's the equivalent of 6,720 times around the world! The lining of the stomach contains 35m glands secreting juices that aid the process of digestion. And these are just a few of the incredibly involved processes and chemical wonders that operate just to sustain life.

As we've seen with the above answer, science and Scripture do not cancel each other out. They simply look at the world from different perspectives, which doesn't automatically mean they contradict each other.

Science cannot prove that God is irrelevant to the universe. If God created it and set the whole thing up, as we believe, He is certainly most relevant! Science has never stopped belief in God and if many great scientists believe - Einstein, Edison, Newton, Boyle, Farriday, Pasteur, Kepler and Copernicus for instance - then that is good enough for me. Eighty years ago, a survey of scientists revealed that 40 per cent believed in God. You might think that with all the scientific breakthroughs and discoveries since that time, this figure might have changed, but an identically worded survey published recently in the journal, *Nature* arrived at almost an identical result - four out of ten scientists believe in God.

Remember, science is about how, Christianity is about why. The crux of the matter is this: the Bible isn't intended to be a science book, instead it's a book about a loving God who created people to have a friendship with. Adam and Eve mucked it up in Genesis, so God sent Jesus to make things right, so we could know Him again ... if we want.

"Science without religion is lame, religion without science is blind."
(Professor Albert Einstein)

SURELY YOU CAN'T BELIEVE THE BIBLE?

We have the English Bible because of English scholars like John Wycliffe and William Tyndale. Tyndale, for example, finally finished translating the Bible into English in July 1525 and throughout his life faced opposition for doing so. His life was full of adventures and narrow escapes, but on October 16 1536, he was finally caught and strangled to death. Then, just for good measure, his body was burnt at the stake. "Forever we're rid of Tyndale", his enemies must have thought, but they were wrong. The product of his labours, the English Bible, is with us today - a book William Tyndale certainly thought was worth dying for.

So what's so special about this book? We've seen already that Christians believe the Bible is the Word of God, and although it was written by men and women, they were inspired by God, meaning that God was the ultimate author. *"All Scripture is given by God and is useful for teaching, for showing people what is wrong in their lives, for correcting faults and for teaching how to live right"* (2 Timothy 3:16).

Researchers in Israel, after subjecting the first five books of the Bible to exhaustive computer analysis, came to a different conclusion than expected. Sceptics had long assumed the Torah (the first five books of the Bible) to have been the work of multiple authors. But Scripture scholar Moshe Katz and computer expert Menachem Weiner of the Israel Institute of Technology, discovered an intricate pattern of significant words in the books, spelled by letters separated at fixed intervals. The statistical possibilities of such patterns happening by chance would be 1 in 3m. The material suggests a single, inspired author - in fact it could not have been put together by human capabilities at all. Mr Weiner adds: "So we need a non-rational explanation. And ours is that the Torah was written by God through the hand of Moses."

The Bible is certainly an amazing book. Sixty-six books in one, written over a 1,500 year period by over forty authors - fishermen, soldiers, kings, peasants, philosophers and even Daniel, a Prime Minister. The Bible was written in three languages: Hebrew, Aramaic and Greek, and includes history books, biographies, poems, songs and even a book of love letters! For all its diversity however, the Bible is a unit. From beginning to end, it tells the story of God's plan for friendship with mankind, which people got wrong, and Jesus made right.

A recent archaeological report in the science magazine, Discovery, contained amazing findings about the Old Testament. Before the discovery of the *Dead Sea Scrolls* in 1947, the oldest Hebrew manuscript dated about 900AD. The *Dead Sea Scrolls*, in startling agreement with the major (Masoretic) text, dated to about 150BC. Yet now archaeologists have discovered a pair of tiny silver scrolls that date back to about 600BC! While digging at the site of a 5th century church in Jerusalem, researchers found a Roman legionnaires' cemetery. Exploring deeper, they found a small burial cave containing the scrolls. Very carefully, less than a millimetre at a time, the scrolls were unrolled. On each of them appeared an excerpt from the book of Numbers that included the word "Jehovah". These scrolls date back to the days before the exile to Babylon, earlier than more sceptical scholars supposed that the Pentateuch (the Torah) had even been written.

I'm realising this answer might be getting a little bit technical so let's finish with what some well-known figures from history have said about the Bible:

"Take all this book you can upon reason, and the balance upon faith, and you will live and die a better man." (Abraham Lincoln - the first President of the USA)

"From early childhood I was taught to appreciate the Bible, and my love for it increases with the passage of time. All through my troubles, I have found it a source of infinite comfort." (Emperor Haile Selassie)

"You Christians have in your keeping a document with enough dynamite in it to blow the whole of civilisation to bits; to turn this world upside down; to bring peace to this worn-torn world. But you read it as if it were just good literature, and nothing else." (Mahatma Gandhi)

11: More Questions

DID JESUS REALLY EXIST?

When you look at the facts, I think you must be a bit daft to believe that Jesus was a sort of fairy story, like *Snow White and the Seven Dwarfs*! Let's examine some of these facts, firstly by looking at the Bible, and then on to other evidence:

The New Testament contains twenty-seven separate books that were all written in the 1st century AD, less than seventy years after Jesus' death. They contain the story of His life and the beginnings of the Christian Church from around 4BC. The facts were recorded by eyewitnesses, who gave first hand accounts of what they had seen and heard. *"We write to you now about what has always existed, which we have heard, we have seen with our own eyes, we have looked at, and we have touched with our hands. We write to you about the Word that gives life"* (1 John 1:1).

Then there's other historical evidence. Josephus, a Jewish historian, wrote this before 100AD: "Now there was about this time Jesus a wise man, if it be lawful to call Him a man; for He was a doer of wonderful works, a teacher of such men as received the truth with pleasure. He drew over to Him many Jews, and also many of the Gentiles. This man was the Christ. And when Pilate had condemned Him to the Cross, those who had loved Him from the first did not forsake Him for He appeared to them alive on the third day, the divine prophets having spoken these and thousands of other wonderful things about Him. And even now, the race of Christians, so named from him, has not died out" *(Antiquities of The Jews, XVIII, III).*

Still want some more evidence? No problem! There is a lot more, but I'll just mention one: Tacitus, a Roman historian, in 112AD writing about the reign of the Emperor Nero, referred to Jesus and the Christians in Rome *(Annals, XV,44)*.

The following famous words about Jesus will help to sum up the life of this incredible man:

He [Jesus] was born in an obscure village, the child of a peasant woman. He grew up in yet another village, where He worked in a carpenter's shop until He was thirty. Then for three years He was an itinerant preacher.

He never wrote a book. He never held an office. He never had a family or owned a big house. He didn't go to college. He never travelled more than 200 miles from the place where He was born. He did none of the things one usually associates with greatness. He had no credentials but Himself.

He was only thirty-three when the tide of public opinion turned against Him. His friends ran away. He was nailed to a Cross between two thieves. While He was dying, His executioners gambled for His clothing, the only property He had on earth.

Nineteen centuries have come and gone and today He is the central figure of the human race. All the armies that ever marched, all the navies that ever sailed, all the parliaments that have ever sat, all the kings that ever reigned, put together, have not affected the life of man on this earth as that one solitary life.

It is a fact that we know more about the life of Jesus than just about any other figure in the ancient world. The bigger question, however, is who was He? There are four options:

1. Lunatic - a mad man who thought He was God. But how did He come back to life?
2. Liar - an evil con-man. But why did He die for a lie?
3. Legend - the whole thing was just a story. But what about the evidence for His life?
4. Lord - He was whom He claimed to be. So what should we do about it?

On one occasion, Michelangelo turned to his fellow artists and said with frustration in his voice: "Why do you keep filling gallery after gallery with endless pictures of Christ in weakness, Christ on the Cross, and most of all, Christ hanging dead? Why concentrate on the passing episode as if it were the last work, as if the curtain dropped down there on disaster and defeat? That dreadful scene only lasted a few hours. But to the unending eternity, Christ is alive, Christ rules and reigns, and triumphs!"

DID JESUS REALLY COME BACK TO LIFE?

The fog lifted. It was June 18 1815, the *Battle of Waterloo*. The French, under the command of Napoleon, were fighting the Allies (British, Dutch and Germans) under the command of Wellington. The people of England depended on a system of signals to find out how the battle was going. One of these signal stations was on the tower of Winchester Cathedral.

Late in the day, it flashed the signal: WELLINGTON DEFEATED. At that very moment, dense fog made it impossible to read the message. The news of defeat quickly spread across the city. The whole countryside was despondent when they heard the news that their country had lost the war. Suddenly the fog lifted, and the remainder of the message could be read. The message had four words, not two. The complete message was: WELLINGTON DEFEATED THE ENEMY. It took only a matter of minutes for the good news to spread. Sorrow was turned into joy, defeat was turned into victory!

It was the same when Jesus was buried in the tomb on that first Good Friday afternoon. Hope had died, even in the hearts of Jesus' best friends. They thought it was all over. They'd only "read" the first part of the message: "Jesus Defeated ..."

The resurrection of Jesus is the cornerstone of Christianity. The Bible even tells us that if Jesus didn't come back to life we are wasting our time: *"And if Christ has not been raised, then your faith has nothing to it"* (1 Corinthians 15:17). Because of His resurrection, Jesus' friends saw the whole picture and could read the completed message: "Jesus Defeated the Enemy". Tragedy had turned to triumph.

On the Friday He was dead, there was no doubt about it. He had been brutally crucified, after which a Roman soldier stuck his spear into His side, to make sure He was dead. The Bible tells us that blood and water poured from the heart. His body was peeled off the Cross and placed in a tomb provided by a wealthy supporter. The grave was guarded, yet on that Sunday He rose again.

Once again, as with these other answers, our belief isn't merely based upon faith or some religious feeling, but upon solid evidence.

Some sceptics have suggested that someone stole His body - but who would do it? Certainly not the Jews or the Romans. Within weeks, all of Jerusalem was talking about rumours that Jesus was alive. Revolution was in the air on the basis of Jesus being alive. If the authorities had the body why didn't they produce it? It is nigh on impossible to believe that the disciples had taken the body. They were terrified and were hiding out of the city. They also later went on to die for their belief that Jesus had come back to life. Why die for a lie, and anyway, how did they get past 100 well trained and disciplined Roman Guards?

Maybe He never died, people say. But think about it: He had been brutally beaten and put through a Roman scourging, He had been pinned up on a cross for six hours with nails in his hands and feet. A spear is rammed into His side, His body taken down and then wrapped in yards of cloth soaked in 34kg of spice. Then three days later, He wakes up and manages to move a 1-2 ton stone in front of His tomb, fight His way past the Roman Guard, and then walk miles to appear to His disciples as the risen Saviour. Need I say any more? What a load of nonsense!

Well, maybe the whole thing was a legend, say others. Looking at the supporting facts, there's no doubt that this was a historical event. When the Garden Tomb was discovered, in 1885, General Gordon and his team were convinced that this was the place where the body of Jesus had lain. There is a traditional tomb inside the wall of the modern Jerusalem, but no certainty attaches to the site. This Garden Tomb, hidden for centuries, was covered with rubbish 20 feet high. When they first cleared the spot, with great caution, they gathered all the dust and debris within the tomb and carefully shipped it to the *Scientific Association of Great Britain*. Every part of it was analysed, but there was no trace of human remains. If this was the real tomb of Jesus, then Jesus was the first to be laid there and He was also the last.

In the early part of the 20th century, a group of lawyers met in England to discuss the Biblical accounts of Jesus' resurrection. They wanted to see if sufficient information was available to make a case that would hold up in an English court of law. When their study was completed, they published the results of their investigations. They concluded that Jesus' resurrection was one of the most well established facts of history.

I read a great short story about the well-known evangelist D. L. Moody, who was asked to preach at a funeral. He hunted throughout the four Gospels, trying to find one of Jesus' funeral sermons, but searched in vain. He found that Jesus disrupted every funeral He ever attended. Death just could not exist where He was. When the dead heard His voice they sprang back to life. Jesus made it quite clear when He said: *"I am the res-urrection and the life"*.

WHAT ABOUT SUFFERING?

This is a really tough question. A little tip here; always be extra espe-cially sensitive when you try to answer this one. Often the questioner is asking this one for personal reasons and has experienced personal tragedy in his or her own life. So always try to delve a little deeper before you ever start to give some sort of answer.

If we're honest, we have to blame ourselves for most of the suffering in this world. Whenever a child is abused, a person murdered, a senior cit-izen mugged you've got to point the finger at the human culprit, not God. Man's inhumanity to man can also be blamed for many of the "natural" disasters we see today. Who can forget Bob Geldof's comments when he saw the devastation caused by the famine in Ethiopia in 1985: "Don't blame God, blame man". For only 200 miles away in the capital Addis Ababa, vast amounts of money were being spent of renovations to the homes of the country's top government officials.

What about earthquakes then - surely you can't blame those on people too? In the beginning, God planned for the world to be so different and for mankind to live in friendship with Him. Hardship and suffering were not on the agenda. We know from what we read in Genesis that God gave peo-ple free will to love Him, and yet people rebelled. The world started to go wrong from that moment. Christians call it "the fall", scientists call it "entropy" - remember the second law of thermodynamics I covered earli-er? The world is in a state of decay and that's why earthquakes, typhoons, whirlwinds, volcanoes and the like cause so much damage today.

God doesn't like suffering either, and He certainly isn't detached or indifferent to it We've looked already at John 3:16, where God sent His one and only begotten Son into the world to save us. The piece, *The Long Silence* explains it like this:

Billions of people were scattered on a great plain before God's throne. Some of the groups near the front talked heatedly - not with cringing shame, but with belligerence. "How can God judge us?", said one.

"What does He know about suffering?" snapped a brunette. She jerked back a sleeve to reveal a tattooed number from a Nazi concentration camp. "We endured terror, beatings, torture and death!"

In another group a black man lowered his collar. "What about this?" he demanded, showing an ugly rope burn. "Lynched for no crime but being black! We have suffocated in slave ships, been wrenched from love ones, toiled till death gave release."

Far out across the plain were hundreds of such groups. Each had a complaint against God for the evil and suffering He permitted in His world. How lucky God was to live in Heaven where there was no weeping, no fear, no hunger, no hatred!

Indeed, what did God know about what man had been forced to endure in this world? "After all, God leads a pretty sheltered life," they said.

So each group sent out a leader, chosen because he had suffered the most. There was a Jew, a black, an untouchable from India, an illegitimate person, a victim of Hiroshima, and one from a Siberian slave camp.

In the centre of the plain, they consulted with each other. At last they were ready to present their case. It was rather simple: before God would be qualified to be their judge, He first must endure what they had endured. Their decision was that God should be sentenced to live on earth - as a man.

But because He was God, they set certain safeguards to be sure He could not use His divine powers to help Himself. Let Him be born a Jew. Let the legitimacy of His birth be doubted, so that none would know who is really His father.

Let Him champion a cause so just, but so radical, that it brings down upon him the hate, condemnation, and efforts of every major traditional and established religious authority to eliminate Him.

Let Him try to describe what no man has ever seen, tasted, heard or smelled - let him try to communicate God to men.

Let Him be betrayed by his closest friends.

Let Him be indicted on false charges, tried before a prejudiced jury, and convicted by a cowardly judge.

Let Him see what it is to be terribly alone and completely abandoned by every living thing.

Let Him be tortured and let Him die! Let Him die the most humiliating death - with common thieves.

As each leader announced his portion of the sentence, loud murmurs of approval went up from the throngs of people.

But when the last had finished pronouncing sentence, there was a long silence. No one uttered a word. No one moved. For suddenly all knew: God had already served his sentence.

That's quite something, isn't it. So let's finish the answer by once again re-focussing on Jesus, and how God wants to know us and help us through life's problems and difficulties. This story is called *Footprints* and it goes like this:

One night a man had a dream. He dreamed he was walking along the beach with the Lord and across the sky flashed scenes from his life. For each scene, he noticed two sets of footprints in the sand; one belonging to him and the other to the Lord.

When the last scene of his life flashed before him, he looked back at the footprints in the sand. He noticed that many times along the path of his life there was only one set of footprints. He also noticed that it happened at the very lowest and saddest times in his life.

This really bothered him and he questioned the Lord about it. "Lord, you said that once I decided to follow you, you'd walk with me all the way. But I have noticed that during the most troublesome times in my life, there is only one set of footprints. I don't understand why when I needed you most, you would leave me."

The Lord replied: "My precious, precious child, I love you and would never leave you. During your times of trial and suffering, when you see only one set of footprints, it was then that I carried you."

What a wonderful encouragement. God is there in the good times and the bad times, because He loves us and wants the best for us, something that is only possible through a personal relationship, available because of what Jesus did through His life, death and resurrection.

12: Even More Questions!

DO MIRACLES STILL HAPPEN?

Many people laugh at the thought that miracles might still happen today. "How can an intelligent person believe it?" "It's just not on - miracles go against the rules of science and nature", are some common remarks.

The very first verse of the Bible starts with the miraculous: *"In the beginning God created the sky and the earth"* (Genesis 1:1). And miracles continue throughout the Bible. Jesus walking on water, feeding 5,000 with five loaves and two fish, healing blind men, casting out demons, and many more miraculous occurrences. Then there's creation, the flood and the parting of the Red Sea.

Over the years, critics have attempted to explain away some of these incidents. For example, some have said, when talking about whether the children of Israel actually went through the parted Red Sea, that there is an area at the north end of the Red Sea called the Bitter Lakes. Between the Bitter Lakes and the Red Sea there was a marshy connection 2-3 inches deep. They say a south-east wind blew up the channel holding the water in the Bitter Lakes, while the tide ebbed away in the Red Sea. So the children of Israel walked through the marshy area.

Now this could be fairly plausible until you start to look at the major weakness in this explanation. If the children of Israel walked across a shallow marshy area, then how did the well-trained Egyptian army drown in 2 inches of water? Now that would have been the miracle!

Just because unusual things sometimes occur outside our understanding and reasoning, that doesn't automatically mean they haven't happened. Here's a few for you, not necessarily miracles but some stories that perhaps show that the impossible can sometimes happen:

With a piercing scream, 29-year-old New Yorker, Elvita Adams, flung herself from the Empire State Building's observation tower, on the 89th floor. Seconds later, she was practically back where she started - plucked from death by a freak up-draught of air. The 30mph gust had whipped her back up the face of the 1,472 feet high skyscraper and dropped her on the 85th floor. Hearing her moans, security guard Frank Clark opened the window and pulled her to safety inside. Elvita, who escaped with very minor injuries and bruises said: "I guess the good Lord didn't mean for me to die just yet."

Mr Thomas Customer, aged 84, faced financial problems when he discovered that his pension and rent books, which he had placed in the oven for safe keeping, had turned to ashes after he forgot to take them out while cooking his lunch. The situation improved the following day, when he won £104,000 on the football pools.

I'm told the chances of getting a complete suit dealt to you at Bridge is 158,753,389,999 to 1. But this actually happened to Bill McNall at the Carlton Club in Gateshead in March 1992. He dealt himself a hand consisting of all thirteen hearts!

Mrs Lois Sattler of Sydney, Australia, sat on top of Pulpit Rock in the Blue Mountains admiring the view. A scene from *Monty Python's Holy Grail* sprang to mind. She turned to a friend and said: "Wouldn't it be funny if God were to strike this mountain." Hardly were the words out of her mouth, than a bolt of lightning zapped out of a suddenly darkened sky and struck her on the behind, tearing the seat out of her jeans. "It's a good job I'm not religious or I might have thought it was very strange," said Mrs Sattler.

Crazy aren't they? But they all happened. I also know miracles happen because I've seen them with my own eyes. I've seen God heal my daughter, Amber, when she was a 7-week-old baby. Amber suddenly started getting very ill and was taken in to hospital for tests. She was so tiny and had become so dehydrated, that it took the doctors 12 hours to put a drip into her. She then underwent a whole series of tests, including blood tests and lumbar punctures to try to find out what was wrong with her. Eventually, X-rays were taken of her tiny stomach and a consultant paediatric surgeon from another hospital came to us with the results. It turned out that her bowel was completely twisted and she needed immediate surgery. We were all taken by ambulance to a specialist children's hospital in Brighton for an operation on her twisted bowel. I took Amber downstairs for a few final X-rays prior to her surgery and watched as tubes were put down her nose, to take the barium (a special mixture that is opaque to X-rays) to examine the damage. We had mobilised our church to pray and I had a lot of faith that God could and would intervene. But even I was surprised when the consultant and his team of two radiographers told me there was nothing wrong with her bowel or stomach any more. Quite simply, God had straightened it all out. I saw the X-rays before and after, and when I told the Surgeon we had been praying and had believed God had performed a miracle, he said: "I am very surprised."

In closing and refocussing, if we take away the miracles from the Bible, there is no real message left. The very heart of Christianity is a miracle, the miracle of God becoming a man in the body of Jesus, who lived, died and came back to life so that we could know friendship with God.

ISN'T IT ALL IN THE MIND?

Some say that Christianity is a kind of psychological crutch - I'm sure we've all heard that one. Well, it is and it isn't.

No, because we've seen from the previous answers that Christianity isn't just a fairy story, or wishful thinking - it's true. Jesus lived and was very real. An anonymous author made this striking comparison:

"Socrates taught for forty years, Plato for fifty, Aristotle for forty, and Jesus for only three. Yet the influence of Christ's three-year ministry infinitely transcends the impact left by the combined 130 years of teaching from these men who were among the great philosophers of all antiquity. Jesus painted no pictures; yet some of the finest paintings of Raphael, Michelangelo and Leonardo da Vinci received their inspiration from Him. Jesus wrote no poetry; but Dante, Milton and scores of the world's greatest poets were inspired by Him. Jesus composed no music; still Haydn, Handel, Beethoven, Bach and Mendelsson reached their highest perfection of melody in the hymns, symphonies and oratorios they composed in His praise. Every sphere of human greatness has been enriched by this humble Carpenter from Nazareth. His unique contribution to the human race is the salvation of the soul! Philosophy could not accomplish that. Nor art. Nor literature. Nor music. Only Jesus Christ can break the enslaving chains of sin and Satan. He alone can speak to the human heart, strengthen the weak and give life to those who are spiritually dead."

At the same time I could say yes, Christianity is a crutch because knowing Jesus helps us through our broken lives - He's there for us. *"God has said, I will never leave you; I will never forget you"* (Hebrews 13:5).

Either way, living a Christian lifestyle certainly isn't an easy option, but I've discovered that it's the best way.

WHAT ABOUT THE OTHER RELIGIONS?

"Don't all roads lead to God?", is a common saying. That's a bit like saying all roads lead to Chichester - what a load of rubbish! The assumption is made that people from all these different religions are experiencing the same God, yet expressing and experiencing it in different ways.

That certainly can't be true. They are all so different. Here is one example for you: *"When you are praying, if you are angry with someone, forgive him so that your Father in heaven will also forgive your sins"* (Mark 11:25).

Powerful words of forgiveness from Jesus. Now compare that quotation with the words of the Ayatollah Khomeini on the same subject of forgiveness, when he was talking about the author, Salman Rushdie on the publication of his controversial book *The Satanic Verses*. "Even if Salman Rushdie repents and becomes the most pious man of time, it is still incumbent on every Moslem to employ everything he's got to send him to hell." Do you notice a subtle difference?

I must say that most religions have elements of truth and some excellent moral teaching. But we need to look at the words of Jesus again: *"I am the way, and the truth, and the life. The only way to the Father is through me"* (John 14:6). Christianity is about a personal relationship with God that is only available through Jesus.

The originator of a new religion came to the great French diplomat and statesman, Charles Maurice de Talleyrand-Perigord and complained that he could not make any converts. "What would you suggest I do?" he asked. "I should recommend," said Telleyrand, "that you get yourself crucified, and then die, but be sure to rise again on the third day."

Christianity is unique because its founder is still alive. When a Muslim goes to Mecca, he will find the grave of Mohammed. That's the difference: Mohammed is dead and in his coffin, and all the other systems of religion and philosophy are in their coffins. But Jesus has risen, and all power in Heaven and on earth is given to Him. Yes, He's alive!

WON'T A GOOD LIFE DO?

Unfortunately, the Bible doesn't allow anyone to earn their way into Heaven. It is great to do good, support charity, be nice to people, and generally be kind and considerate. But the Bible makes it clear: our good deeds, while being very admirable, don't actually bring us into a relationship with God. *"It was not because of good deeds we did to be right with him. He saved us through the washing that made us new through the Holy Spirit"* (Titus 3:5).

I'll tell you why good works aren't enough. Look at God's standard. It's perfection and none of us can reach it. Even if we've never murdered anyone or stolen goods from the supermarket, however good we think we might be, we don't come up to God's standard of perfection. Paul, when writing to the Christians in Rome, makes it crystal clear: *"all have sinned and are not good enough for God's glory"* (Romans 3:23). Bad news isn't it? But he goes on to tell us: *"and all need to be made right with God by his grace, which is a free gift. They need to be made free from sin through Jesus Christ"* (Romans 3:24).

The TV presenter, Anne Diamond, said on her daytime television programme on the subject of belief: "It doesn't matter what you believe, as long as you are sincere." I've got to say, and apologies to you if you're currently reading this book Anne, that that is utter rubbish. Sincerity has nothing to do with it. What if you happen to be sincerely wrong; does that make things right? I'm sure Adolf Hitler, in his own mind, was very sincere about wishing to create a master race, and annihilating 6m Jews. But look at the devastating results - he was most definitely sincerely wrong.

Sincerity and doing good simply aren't enough. This means good and bad people both need Jesus all the same - whoever you are, whatever you've done, Jesus is the only way.

So there we are, the top twelve questions that most people ask. But what about questions that you just can't answer? That's quite simple: admit that you don't know but will find out. I'm sure you've met some of those irritating people who think they know everything about every subject you might care to mention: I find them very annoying. If you really don't know the answer, there's no need to bluff your way through, or to skilfully avoid the question altogether, as we've all seen politicians do from time to time. Make a note of the question and find the answer, from a more experienced Christian or a book, or do the research yourself; but promise to get back to the questioner. It also gives you the opportunity to spend more time with them.

13: Leading Someone to Christ

So now you've come to that wonderful moment when a person wants to make a commitment. They obviously need to understand the key points of the Gospel and be ready to take it on board.

It's time to make the big introduction. I've found that this is a step which many Christians are scared to take. Imagine this: a salesman in an electrical store shows you a brand new TV, just out on the market, half the price of its competitors, guaranteed for life, quality far superior to anything you've ever seen. It would look just perfect in your lounge. Remote control, stereo surround sound - the lot. He tells you it's the best thing since sliced bread and you agree. But then he says goodbye and walks off. You're left standing there scratching your head, thinking to yourself: "I want one, but how do I get it?"

In a similar way, people are often ready to respond to what we've told them about the Gospel. But we often don't - through embarrassment or fear of them saying "no". Give them the chance. Of course sometimes they might say no, but many, many times they will say "yes".

If they do say "no", well that's their prerogative. Do make sure they've understood what you've said, but don't push it. At the end of the day it's their decision. If Jesus respected people's individual freedom, I think we should too.

It might be that it's just too much for them to take in in one go. They may want to think about it for a day or so. Great, but do something that will actually make them think more about it. Lend them a book or some literature, and arrange to collect it in 24-hours.

And of course, if they're still not interested in Jesus or becoming a

Christian, don't stop being friends with them. Some Christians just see the unsaved as "pew-fodder", or numbers to chalk up on their Bible. That's not on at all. I've known my mate Graham since we started going to the same school together at the age of five. Humanly speaking, he is nowhere near becoming a Christian, but he's still my mate and he always will be, even if he never becomes a Christian.

When they do say "yes", make sure you introduce them to Jesus then and there. How you actually pray is really up to you. You might like to pray a prayer of commitment, and simply ask the person to agree by saying "Amen" at the end. The person might want to pray it themselves, maybe reading a written prayer from a book or Gospel tract. Or you could do it the way I like to, whereby I pray the prayer a line at a time, asking the person to repeat it after me, either out loud or silently in their head. If you do the latter, don't race through it in all your excitement. Give them time to pray the line after you've said it.

As for the content of your prayer, I've included a "model" prayer at the end of this chapter. But here are the points you need to cover. It's even easier than last time to remember, in fact it's as simple as A,B,C.

ADMIT

A person needs to admit that they've done wrong, that they have sinned. That they have gone their own selfish way instead of God's way. The Bible uses the word "repentance", which literally means a deep sorrow about your actions and a turning away from all you know to be wrong. In fact, to say sorry and to be sorry (Romans 3:23; 6:23).

BELIEVE

The person needs to believe that Jesus' dying on the Cross and resurrection was the ultimate sacrifice, and made it possible for us to start a new life. He paid the price for the death penalty our sins deserved (John 3:16; 1 Peter 3:18).

COMMIT

Now it's time for them to commit themselves to living God's way, from this point onwards - to become a Christian. When you think about it logically, it's stupid to live any other way. God created us, so He knows what's best for us. Remember, the advice we often see on all sorts of products: "for best results follow the maker's instructions". He won't leave us to it though, He'll help us too! If we put God in charge of our lives, He promises to live inside us, by his Holy Spirit, which gives us power to change and get to know God. *"But to all who did accept him and believe in him he gave the right to become children of God"* (John 1:12).

THE PRAYER

Dear Father God,

I am really sorry for all my sins, for all the things I've done, said and thought that were wrong. I choose to turn from those things and live my life your way. I believe that Jesus died on a cross to set me free, so I could know you. Please come into my life and fill me with your Holy Spirit, so as from today I can start to live my life in a way that pleases Jesus.

Amen.

Afterwards, always remember to ask the person how they feel. They might be expecting some sort of "Saul on the road to Damascus experience", complete with blinding lights and voices from Heaven, and might be disappointed or confused if it doesn't happen to them. They might feel different, or they might not, and you need to explain this to them. After all, the Christian faith is built upon belief, and not necessarily feelings all the time.

"Here I am! I stand at the door and knock. If you hear my voice and open the door, I will come in and eat with you, and you will eat with me" (Revelation 3:20).

14: Making Disciples

When a person becomes a Christian, they have been "born again" (John 3:3). The old has gone and God has given them a fresh start, so they most certainly need our help. You shouldn't need to change nappies or physically feed them, but they will need other help as they grow as a Christian.

To be honest with you, I had a hard time after I became a Christian. No one ever really helped me much at all. I was given some Bible reading notes but that was about it. I didn't really grow much for at least five years. One day I explained to the minister of my church that I had been filled with the Holy Spirit and he told me that sort of thing didn't happen to people anymore, it was only for establishing the early Church. It was all very confusing to say the least! My mate Geoff took me under his wing though, and visits to a local lively Baptist church on a Sunday night, followed by a chat, coffee and pancakes in the cafe up the road, kept me going through those hard times in my Christian life. In time I found a great, lively church where I finally started to grow, at long last.

The Bible uses a word for this whole process of growing in God - discipleship. You see, Jesus never told us to go and make Christians. He was very clear: *"Therefore, go and make disciples of all nations, baptising them in the Father and of the Son and of the Holy Spirit, and teaching them to obey everything I have commanded you"* (Matthew 28:18-20). If we look even closer at the original text, we can see that it probably is more likely to imply, "as you are going, as you are teaching, as you are baptising, make disciples".

This process of disciple-making is highly important, because it's an integral part of "The Great Commission". The word for disciple - "math-etes" - actually means "learner", a learner by use and practice. The word mathematics (I hope that doesn't bring back too many horrific memories from your school days!), the subject regarded by ancient scholars as the essential building block to all learning, comes directly from this word.

The modern equivalent of mathetes would be the word "apprentice", a master craftsman passing on his skills and the tricks of the trade to someone else. People often ask me how I became an escapologist. I bought some books that Houdini wrote and read them over and over again and picked up a load of theoretical information. But that didn't make me an escape artist. I didn't become an escape artist until an experienced escape artist showed up and then taught me how to actually get out of a strait -jacket. In other words, not just head knowledge but practical side-by-side instruction.

Once again, and it's not terribly surprising really, Jesus was the expert at this sort of thing. He was the undisputed master craftsman with a group of young apprentices. The verb to disciple - "manthano" - occurs only twenty-five times in the New Testament (just six times in the Gospels). The noun disciple - "mathetes" - occurs 264 times exclusively in the Gospels and the book of Acts.

History books are full of stories of gifted people whose talents were overlooked by a procession of people, until someone believed in them. Einstein was four-years-old before he could speak and seven before he could read. Isaac Newton did poorly in school. A newspaper editor fired Walt Disney because he had "no good ideas." Leo Tolstoy dropped out of college, and the renowned mathematician, Werner von Braun, failed alge-bra at school. Haydn gave up ever making a musician of Beethoven, who seemed a slow and plodding young man with no apparent talent - except a belief in music.

So a disciple is a follower of Jesus, a person who is eager to learn and apply the truths that Jesus taught, which results in a deeper commitment to follow Him and His ways. The verb "to disciple" describes the process by which a person is encouraged by another more experienced person to be such a follower of Jesus. It includes different methods to help the per-son to become mature as a Christian and so, in time, they can go on to dis-ciple others.

You can see that this discipleship business is most certainly very pow-erful stuff, but how do we actually do it more effectively? Let's look at Jesus' model:

SPENDING TIME

Bible scholars point out that the synoptic gospels cover only thirty-three or thirty-four days of Jesus' three year ministry, and John only records eighteen days. So what did He do the rest of the time? Jesus strategy was to concentrate His time on training His disciples, rather than speaking to large crowds. Quite simply, He wanted to be with them, they were His spiritual children. As a father myself, I have found this to be true. The best way to properly raise a family is to be with them.

In the same way, we must learn to spend quality time with new converts, mixing social and spiritual together in a very natural way. Teach them the basics of growth by showing them how to pray and get the best out of the Bible. Let's face it, if we're honest, we probably all find Bible study and prayer a bit of a struggle, so teach them from your mistakes, show them what works for you. These things are a discipline, so why not do them together and help each other grow.

GIVING HIMSELF AWAY

Jesus continually gave Himself away. Someone once said that most things are caught and not just taught. The disciples caught His enthusiasm and heartbeat for the lost. Evangelism was a compulsion for Him, and in time His vision became their vision.

Church can be intimidating for new Christians, with its unfamiliar songs and surroundings, strange jargon, and lots of new faces. You need to put yourself out as Jesus did. Don't expect the new convert to turn up alone. I suggest you pick them up, bring them with you and look after them. Don't leave them when you both get to the meeting, and then drift around with your friends. Stick with them and involve them, and introduce them to a handful of your more normal Christian friends. Explain what's happening during the meeting, and take them back for lunch afterwards and talk through the meeting. I'll say it again: put yourself out and give yourself away.

GAVE THEM THINGS TO DO

Finally, Jesus assigned His disciples jobs to do, to put into practice what they had heard Him say and observed Him do. They had been with him, he had prayed for them and now this was His plan for them to do the same. This was His strategy to win the world.

New Christians can be the most effective witnesses, and that's a fact. They probably know more unbelievers than you do, so make the most of it. Show them how to be a witness, let them see how you evangelise. Share your heart and share the vision, and get them doing it.

Dr James Kennedy, founder of *Evangelism Explosion*, talks about discipleship in a very graphic way. He makes the point that if you were an outstanding international evangelist and won 1,000 people a night for the Lord, it would take you 16,438 years to reach the whole world of 6 billion people for Jesus. However, if you were discipling the Jesus way, and if you were able to win just one person a year and could train that person to win one other person each year, and so on, it would take just thirty-three years to win the whole world for Jesus.

So, in conclusion, how do we practically go about making better disciples?

1. Invest time with people
2. Give yourself away
3. Share your heart
4. Share your vision
5. Pray for them
6. Take them with you
7. Let them watch you at work
8. Watch them at work
9. Let them do the work themselves
10. Give them new challenges and achievable goals

15: Power for Evangelism

There was a successful mission in Bournemouth some years ago, which the evangelist Ian Coffee fronted, called *He's Here*. It was subtitled *A natural look at a supernatural God*. Ian was great, and large numbers of people became Christians, but I always wondered how it might have been different if instead of being a "natural look" it could have been a "supernatural look at a supernatural God". There's no doubt about it: signs and wonders have a funny way of making people sit up and take notice.

Just before Jesus ascended into Heaven, He told His disciples not to leave Jerusalem until they received the Holy Spirit. This Holy Spirit would give them the power they needed for their mission. You see, God always gives us the tools we need for the job. *"When the Holy Spirit comes to you, you will receive power. You will be my witnesses - in Jerusalem, in all of Judea, in Samaria and in every part of the world"* (Acts 1:8).

After Jesus death, His disciples ran away and hid, totally demoralised. The book of John shows them huddled together in a room, locked away for fear of what their enemies would do to them. They thought the whole plan had gone wrong, and they were part of its failure.

Into this setting, the resurrected Jesus came and said: *"Peace be with you."* After He said this, He showed them His hands and side and proved to them it was Him and He had come back from the dead. Then He said it again: *"Peace be with you. As the Father sent me, I now send you."* After he said this, he breathed on them and said: *"Receive the Holy Spirit"* (John 20:19-22).

Consider the change in these men just a few weeks later. Jesus had ascended into Heaven and the Apostles were in Jerusalem for a festival called Pentecost. Now Pentecost before the birth of the Church was a major time of celebration amongst the Jews. The festivities revolved around celebrating the wheat harvest and they ate, drank, and were generally quite merry!

It was then that the Holy Spirit came to empower those timid men: *"When the day of Pentecost came, they were all together in one place. Suddenly a noise like a strong, blowing wind came from heaven and filled the whole house where they were sitting. They saw something like flames of fire that were separated and stood over each person there. They were all filled with the Holy Spirit, and they began to speak different languages by the power the Holy Spirit was giving them"* (Acts 2:1-4).

Not surprisingly, this drew a bit of crowd, and the religious people who were watching this holy commotion thought that they'd had a little too much wine to say the least. Peter, indignant at the jibes and ridicule, stood up, full of the Holy Spirit and preached one heck of an evangelistic sermon. And 3,000 got saved in one go! (Acts 2:14-42) What a change in Peter!

A little while later, Peter and John on their way to their daily prayer meeting at the Temple, saw a blind man who asked them for money. Look at Peter's response: *"I don't have any silver or gold, but I do have something else I can give you. By the power of Jesus Christ from Nazareth, stand up and walk!"* (Acts 3:6) Peter physically grabbed him and pulled him up, and this once crippled man started walking and jumping and praising God.

Not surprisingly, this sort of thing drew a crowd again, and the next day the Jewish rulers, elders and teachers of the law called them in for questioning. Peter, once again full of the Holy Spirit, said to them: *"... are you questioning us about a good thing that was done to a crippled man? Are you asking us who made him well? We want all of you and all the Jewish people to know that this man was made well by the power of Jesus Christ from Nazareth. You crucified him, but God raised him from the dead. This man was crippled, but he is now well and able to stand here before you because of the power of Jesus"* (Acts 4:8-10).

It goes on that the Jewish leaders saw Peter and John's boldness, even though they weren't educated or had special training and they were amazed. *"Then they realised that Peter and John had been with Jesus"* (Acts 4:13).

For the other Apostles, it was the same. After Saul met with Jesus on the way to Damascus, he *"preached fearlessly in the name of Jesus"* (Acts 9:27). We also read about Barnabus and Paul speaking boldly for the Lord. These once terrified men, had experienced a powerful encounter with God, and they each went on to suffer extreme persecution and often-death for the glorious message of a Gospel they just couldn't keep silent about. *"We cannot keep quiet. We must speak about what we have seen and heard"* (Acts 4:20). Legend tells us that the disciples all preferred to suffer greatly, rather than to refute their faith.

Matthew became a martyr when he was slain with a sword in Ethiopia.

Mark eventually died after being cruelly dragged through the streets.

Luke was hanged from an olive tree in Greece.

John was put in a cauldron of boiling oil, but survived miraculously, and was banished to Patmos.

Peter was crucified upside down in Rome.

James the Greater was beheaded in Jerusalem.

James the Less was thrown from the top of the temple, and then beaten to death with a fuller's club.

Philip was hanged up against a pillar at Heiropolis in Phrygia.

Bartholomew was flayed alive.

Andrew was bound to a cross, where he preached to his persecutors until he died.

Thomas was run through the body with a lance at Coromandel in the East Indies.

Jude was shot to death with arrows.

Matthias was first stoned, and then beheaded.

Barnabus was stoned to death by the Jews at Salonica.

Paul after various tortures and persecutions, was at length beheaded at Rome by the Emperor Nero.

You see, God impacted these once frightened men with His power, the Holy Spirit. The Good News is, this same power is with us today. The Greek word for power is "dunamis", which is where we get our English word "dynamite". We all know what explosive damage a stick of dynamite will do. This dunamis is also an explosive power that changes things. Just look what Jesus said: *"And those who believe will be able to do these things as proof"* (Mark 16:17). As I've said before, signs and wonders have a funny way of attracting attention.

I had been working in sunny Herne Bay in Kent for a long weekend in November (when it wasn't terribly sunny and in fact was rather bleak!), and myself and a friend wandered down to the sea front to do some detached youth work. We were chatting away to a large gang of lads about all sorts, and were gradually steering the conversation onto our relationship with God. Well, this guy Simon pulled his sleeve up to reveal a badly scarred arm. "Here mate, if your God is so great He can heal my arm." I was wondering if it was a question or a challenge. I figured I had nothing to lose, apart from looking a bit of an idiot (and I can cope with that), so I got all the lads standing round in a circle as I prayed for Simon's injured arm. I really did have a lot of faith, and the story would read a lot better if I said his arm was miraculously healed then and there, and they all got saved. But instead I'll be honest - nothing happened!

Well, I was a little bit down about the whole situation, but I felt I had been obedient to God, so there wasn't a lot more I could do. The next evening we returned to the beach. Simon saw us across the road and started shouting: "Oi, mate [he never did seem to get around to remembering my name], your God has made my arm better." He came over and showed us his unblemished, unmarked arm, which in turn drew a larger crowd than the night before, all that with one person becoming a Christian! And I could tell you many other stories like this. From what I read of the New Testament - and feel free to disagree - I am convinced that signs and wonders were for the un-churched, those who weren't Christians, "as proof" (Mark 16:17), and that they are still today.

It does work, so start taking a few risks. Here's a check-list to help you get started praying with more power and seeing the miraculous released to unbelievers:

1. Have faith - know that God wants to start healing this person now (Isaiah 53:5; Matthew 10:7-8)
2. Check your motives - don't feel pressured and don't pray out of guilt (Romans 14:23)
3. Don't put the person under pressure - if they don't want it that's fair enough
4. Relax and be normal - please don't get all religious about it
5. Listen to God - see what He wants to say in this situation, He may give you "keys" to unlock things
6. Don't rush it - even Jesus didn't always crack it first time (Mark 8:22-25)
7. Don't blame the person's lack of faith if nothing happens
8. Do raise their faith expectations - help them to believe, and always point them to Jesus
9. Speak with authority to the sickness - break its hold and pray in the healing power of God

10. Lay hands on the person - as you do so the Holy Spirit and blessing is imparted. Don't feel you need to lay hands on their head, whilst talking loudly in tongues in the middle of Tesco though! It will look a bit odd. Why not just touch their arm, or hold their hands. It's a lot more normal and yes, it does still work!

"I am not ashamed of the Gospel, because it is the power of God - for the salvation of everyone who believes" (Romans 1:16).

16: Getting Going

In 1946, California lawyer Richard M. Nixon answers an advertisement in a newspaper and is launched on his political career. The ad read: "Wanted: Congressional candidate with no previous political experience to defeat a man who has represented the district in the House for ten years. Any young man, resident of the district, preferably a veteran, may apply for the job". Richard Nixon of course went on to become president of the United States of America.

We all qualify for the job of evangelism. We should all apply, for the Bible tells us to. I hope this book has been helpful and practical and not too technical. But you really don't need to master everything in its pages before you start witnessing - it's time to get going now.

Have a look at how the apostle Matthew got started: *"When Jesus was leaving, he saw a man named Matthew sitting in his tax collector's booth. Jesus said to him, 'Follow me,' and he stood up and followed Jesus. As Jesus was having dinner at Matthew's house, many tax collectors and "sinners" came and ate with Jesus and his followers. When the Pharisees saw this, they asked Jesus' followers, 'Why does your teacher eat with tax collectors and sinners?' When Jesus heard them, he said, 'It is not the healthy people who need a doctor, but the sick. Go and learn what this means: "I want kindness more than I want animal sacrifices". I did not come to invite good people but to invite sinners'"* (Matthew 9:9-13).

Jesus had chosen Matthew the tax-collector to be an Apostle. You can read the parallel passages in Mark and Luke where Matthew is called Levi (because the authors tried to disguise Matthew's job prior to his conversion), as tax collectors were so hated. Palestine was a country subject to the Romans and tax collectors were employed by the Romans and were therefore regarded as traitors. The whole taxation was very complex, but I won't bore you with details of the poll tax, which all men from the ages of 14 to 65, and all women from 12 to 65, had to pay just for existing. Or the ground tax that consisted of one-tenth of all grain grown, and one-fifth of wine and oil; and then income tax of 1 per cent of a man's income. If all that wasn't enough there were all kind of duties. A tax was payable for using the main roads, the harbours, and markets. A tax was payable on a cart, on each wheel of it, and on the animal that drew it. There was a pur-chase tax on certain articles, and there were import and export duties. I could go on, and you thought our current taxes were unfair!

It is absolutely true to say that murderers, robbers and tax-collectors were classed together; yet Jesus chose Matthew to be an Apostle. This must have been a huge sacrifice for Matthew, for he must have been very wealthy, and indeed must have been the richest of the Disciples. The fish-ermen could have returned to their trade without too much difficulty, but for Matthew his job was over, even if he wanted to return to it - he had abandoned his tax job once and for all.

He didn't seem to have any regrets about it though. He wanted everyone to know about it. I love what Matthew did when Jesus "called" him. Matthew invited Jesus to a slap-up meal at his house, and invited his friends and work colleagues too, so that they could meet Jesus. His first instinct was to share with his friends what he had found - isn't that wonderful?

And that is what we need to do. We need to start effectively telling others who we have found. I know that to have read this far, you must be concerned about evangelism, otherwise you wouldn't have started in the first place. So that's good enough motivation for starters. Begin where it is relatively easy to speak about Jesus. Don't go to the seediest night-club in town and stand up and do a ten-minute presentation in the middle of the dance floor (unless God has told you to!). That's probably not the wis-est place to begin. Instead, start where it's easier.

Jesus talked about *soil* that had been prepared for the good seed of the Gospel (Matthew 13:1-43). He was talking about people who are ready to respond, a much better and more encouraging way to start. Why not vol-unteer to be part of a counselling team at an evangelistic event, so when people respond to the message of the Gospel it's over to you to lead them to the Lord.

I mentioned earlier about my year of training in evangelism. I spent a lot of time in the classroom learning the theory, but learned the practice out on the road with someone who was far more experienced than me.

Jesus showed His disciples this principle of seeing and doing as He sent them out to do the work they'd seen Him doing: *"So the apostles went out and travelled through all the towns, preaching the Good News and healing people everywhere"* (Luke 9:6). I would strongly recommend you try to do the same, by identifying a person who has specific evangelistic gifting and asking if you can spend time with them. This Biblical formula goes like this:

1. The master works, the disciple watches him work - you watch him
2. Then the disciple works with the master - you work together
3. The disciple works, the master watches - he watches you at work
4. The disciple becomes the master - he then finds someone else to disciple

This is a key step. As the ancient Chinese proverb goes: "I hear - I forget, I see - I remember, I do - I understand".

The final step to getting going is prayer. There's an old saying that goes something like this: you get specific answers when you pray specific prayers. Vague prayers get vague answers, so let's get specific. Why not make a list. Here's some suggestions, not necessarily in order:

1. Identify up to five people you know who aren't Christians
2. Start praying for special things for each of them
3. Plan some friendship activities you know you'll both enjoy
4. Spend quality time together
5. Start introducing them to some of your Christian friends
6. Tell them about some of the activities your Church is putting on that might be suitable for them
7. Give them a good quality Christian book that will intrigue them a little more
8. Tell them your story
9. Invite them to church
10. Tell them about the Gospel

A survey was taken in 1989 of people who were over the age of 95. They were all asked one question, and it was deliberately left open-ended so they could answer any way they wished. The question was: If you could live your life over again, what would you do differently? Among all the different answers, these three replies came back most frequently:

1. If I could live my life over again, I would reflect more
2. I would risk more
3. I would do more things that would live on after I'm dead

In New Testament times, the ratio of Christians to unbelievers of the population was 1 to 360. That means quite simply that every Christian would have to personally lead 360 people to the Lord to see the whole world saved. Since that time the world has expanded, the population increased, new countries and people groups have been discovered, and the Gospel has gone literally to the ends of the earth. This ratio, according to my friends at Links International, has now drastically reduced to an astonishing 1:6.8. That means that if each of us reached just seven people, the whole world would be saved.

It's astonishing isn't it? Just seven people each! But let's not just reflect on these things. Let's start taking risks to see this achievable goal reached, and learn to pass it on to others so that the dream and motivation lives on. It really can be done if we all get on with the task that God has called us to. So it's crunch time - it is actually time to get started. Make your first step, even if it's only a small one - don't miss out, you could really live to regret it.

17: Seizing the Day

In the hit movie the *Dead Poet's Society*, Robin Williams played the role of a teacher in an exclusive American prep school. On the first day of school, he takes the class of boys out into the hallway to look at the pictures of past, now dead, graduates of the school. He motivates them to learn and excel in life with the following words:

"We are food for worms lads! Believe it or not, each and every one of us in this room one day will stop breathing, turn cold and die. Step forward and see these faces from the past. They were just like you are now. They believe they're destined for great things. Their eyes are full of hope. But, you see, gentlemen, these boys are now fertilising daffodils. If you listen close, you will hear them whisper their legacy to you. Lean in. What do you hear?" Then Williams says in a spooky, grave-like voice: "Carpe Diem! [Latin for seize the day] Seize the day boys! Make your lives extraordinary!"

What advice that is for us as Christians! Let's seize the day while we can; let's take our villages, towns, cities and nations for God, making a difference and being good news to all those we know and meet. Let's begin changing things for good.

Evangelism is like driving a car: it can only be learned by doing it. You will not be able to drive if you sit at home with your feet up memorising The Highway Code all day. You need to get in the car and learn to drive.

It's now the end of the book and it's time to get in the car and join millions of other "drivers" out there, shouting "turn the key, get your foot down and get going!"

Your journey's start in sharing your faith might not be a big one.

Indeed your start might not move you very far at all. But at least you are moving forward. Remember what God has said: *"Go and make followers of all people in the world"* (Matthew 28:19).

Wonderful things are currently happening in our world. There are more Christians alive today than ever in the whole of history added together. Every single day 100,000 people around the world give their lives to Jesus, and 2,000 new churches are planted each week. In 1992, I had the great privilege of working alongside evangelist Reinhard Bonnke during the Eurofest Festival in Birmingham. Reinhard's battle cry is "Africa shall be saved", and every day in that massive continent, 20,000 become Christians.

In South Korea, home of the largest church in the world, there are now 18,000,000 Christians out of a total population of 44,000,000 - that's nearly a massive 41 per cent of the entire country. In China, 28,000 people become Christians every day, and it is estimated that in the last seventeen years an incredible 80,000,000 have turned to Jesus. Things are happening at such a pace there are now more Christians in China than there are members of the Communist Party - indeed some of China's best evangelists are only aged 14 and 15.

The New York Times, in May 1997, reported "Revival is breaking out in Pensacola, Florida". Since 1995, the Brownsville Assembly of God church has attracted thousands of people. It has turned into the largest and longest-running Pentecostal revival in America this century. The *Pensacola Outpouring*, as it is known, has been drawing between 3,000 and 6,000 people a night to the small church, and the pastoral staff say that as of May 16 1997, 107,000 people had signed visitor's cards saying that they had been saved. Ushers told *The New York Times* that as many as three times that number had answered the nightly altar-calls.

The Pensacola revival has been attracting all sorts of people: Muslims have been converted, a busload of gang members from Chicago have become Christians, people who barely speak English have responded to the call and even a coven of witches from New Orleans went to the church. The extraordinary events started on Father's Day 1995, and began when a visiting speaker was in full flow speaking about "burning hell". The congregation were reported to be weeping and repenting when a great wind buffeted the altar. Since then things have never been the same.

So there we have it; some amazing stories to wet your appetite. Yes, God is doing wonderful things across our world. Let's be part of it, and get on with our essential role in reaching our nations for Jesus.

I'm going to leave the last words to Paul, who once revealed a side of himself that surprised the Christians in Corinth, when he came to them *"in weakness and fear, and with much trembling"*.

> *"Continue praying, keeping alert and always thanking God. Also pray for us that God will give us an opportunity to tell people his message. Pray that we can preach the secret that God has made known about Christ. This is why I am in prison. Pray that I can speak in a way that will make it clear, as I should. Be wise in the way you act with people who are not believers, making the most of every opportunity. When you talk, you should always be kind and pleasant so you will be able to answer everyone in the way you should"* (Colossians 4:2-6).

Breakout!

Steve Legg is available on a national and international basis for evangelistic events, including schools, colleges and university work, street theatre, cabarets, special church guest meetings and after dinner entertainment. He is also able to lead practical training seminars on the topics covered in *Making Friends*. For more information, please contact Steve at the following address:

The Breakout Trust
PO Box 3070
LITTLEHAMPTON
West Sussex BN17 5AW
UNITED KINGDOM